BEATRICE

*The Cadbury Heiress Who Gave
Away Her Fortune*

FIONA JOSEPH

FOXWELL PRESS

Copyright © Fiona Joseph 2012

First published by
Foxwell Press
1301 Stratford Road
Hall Green
Birmingham
B28 9HH

ISBN 978-0-9570934-0-9

A CIP catalogue record for this book is available from the British Library.

Typeset in Garamond by print.uk.net.
Cover design by Stuart Bache
Book design by Adam Davis

A Kindle edition of this book is also available:
ISBN 978-0-9570934-1-6

Cover images courtesy of the Bournville Archive.
Front cover: Beatrice Cadbury (top) and the Bournville Works in the 1880s (bottom)
Back cover: The Boeke Family in 1925. Left to right: Helen, Emma, Kees, Candia, Beatrice, Daniel, Theodora, Julia and Paula.

For Peter and our girls, Anna and Stella

Contents

Prologue
September 1920, Bilthoven, Holland

IN A SIMPLE but large detached villa in the tranquil town of Bilthoven, an Englishwoman – known to locals as Betty Boeke – sat with her Dutch husband, Kees, and composed a letter to her eldest brother in England. It was two years since this couple in their mid-thirties had moved from their Birmingham home to this house, which was set back from the lane and surrounded by a forest of tall pine trees. A wooden plaque above the front door bore the name *Het Boschhuis* – the house in the woods.

Inside, the décor was plain, without frills or ornamentation. The stone floors were covered by a small rug here and there, but no portraits or paintings adorned the walls. In the main living room the few items of furniture could be counted on one hand – a single sofa, a bookcase, Kees's piano and a long farmhouse table with wooden chairs. Alone on the mantelpiece the serene open-armed figure of Thorwaldson's *Christ* seemed to be watching over Betty as she gathered her thoughts. On first appearances, it was a room belonging to a married couple on limited means who, while not exactly hard-up, had no money for fancy extras.

And yet a sharp-eyed onlooker would have detected clues of

hidden wealth and status in that sparsely furnished room. Had they been drawn to stroke the polished rosewood lid of the piano, for instance, they might have been surprised to see the logo of C. Bechstein, the famous Berlin manufacturer whose instruments could be found in concert halls and private mansions all over Europe. Lying atop the piano there was a black case. Inside it was Betty's engagement present to Kees nine years before – a violin from one of the finest violin and bow makers of the era, William Hill & Sons of London. Elsewhere in the house, there were further signs of affluence, including the well-stocked library in the adjoining room that was home to countless books, many of them valuable first editions.

For all Betty's attempts to furnish *Het Boschhuis* in a simple manner consistent with her Quaker beliefs, she could neither disguise nor escape the fact that she was a very rich woman. Unbeknown to many Bilthoven residents, Betty Boeke was, in fact, the daughter of one of England's most successful Victorian entrepreneurs – Richard Cadbury of Cadbury Brothers. Richard and his younger brother, George, had built their chocolate-making factory at Bournville on the outskirts of Birmingham, and Richard's generous legacy to the family, following his untimely death, ensured Betty would never want for money for the rest of her life. Since the age of twenty-one, Betty had been a shareholder in the Cadbury firm, but, instead of revelling in a lifestyle of pampered privilege, that wealth was making Betty increasingly troubled.

Now, after many months of earnest thought and heartfelt discussion, it was time to do something about it.

*

Out in the nearby woods, the four Boeke girls roamed, playing their usual games of hide-and-seek and collecting pine cones as a present for their mother. Helen, almost eight, was in charge, although six-year-old Emma was a loyal second-in-command. Next came Paula, aged four, followed by Julia, three, trailing unsteadily behind her sisters. With their long white-blonde hair they looked like angels. They were a lively bunch and chattered away in a mixture of Dutch and English. A fifth child, baby Candia, being only five months old lay sleeping in a wooden crib at her mother's side.

Betty knew that the decision she was about to announce to her brother would irrevocably affect her, Kees and their girls, and also throw down a challenge to the Cadbury firm. But her sense of conviction was strong and Kees was fully behind her.

On a sheet of blue letter-headed notepaper she wrote the date – 27th September 1920. After the briefest of pauses, the words began to flow.

'Dear Barrow,

I do not expect thou wilt be so very much surprised at receiving this as thou know the whole question has been in our minds for a long time now …

I have felt increasing difficulty [she continued] at receiving year by year the income from our Bournville shares, as we did nothing to earn this money, and it only came to us through inheritance.'

She quickly filled the rest of the page, outlining the course of action she wanted Barrow to take on her behalf. When she had finished, she signed it, 'Thy loving sister, Beatrice', and then sealed the letter, ready for posting in the morning.

*

Barrow Cadbury was Beatrice's eldest brother, or half-brother to be precise. Richard Cadbury's first wife Elizabeth, Barrow's mother, had died when Barrow was only six. Richard remarried quickly and soon Barrow and his other siblings were to have four half-sisters: Edith, Helen, Daisy and little Beatrice. Barrow was twenty-three by the time Beatrice was born in 1884 and he had already joined his father Richard and Uncle George helping to manage the Bournville Works factory.

In family circles Barrow and Beatrice were known as 'Big B' and 'Little B' and he had a particular affection for his youngest sister when she was growing up. Known for his prudence, Barrow kept savings accounts for each of his younger sisters to encourage them to develop sound financial habits. (At the same time, he could not resist adding extortionate amounts of 'interest' to their bank books, from his own pocket.) This mixture of thrift and generosity was legendary at the Bournville Works too. In 1897, Barrow had established a savings scheme for Cadbury employees to celebrate Queen Victoria's diamond jubilee; every employee with over three years' service was given twenty shillings, with ten shillings for those who had been employed under three years. On their father's death in 1899, the Cadbury Brothers partnership became a limited company. Barrow was made company secretary and served as a director, along with the second eldest brother, William, and his two cousins. Now, in 1920, Barrow Cadbury was approaching sixty but still full of vigour with a firm and steady hand needed for the commercial business environment.

He was at his home in the suburbs of Birmingham, when Beatrice's letter arrived one early October morning. Along with the letter, written in his sister's distinctive forward-sloping hand, there was another enclosure running to five pages. The top of that document was headed with the words: 'To all who are co-operating in the Works known as Cadbury Brothers, Ltd., Bournville'. Would her brother be kind enough, Beatrice asked, to have the document typed up, printed and distributed to every employee at the factory?

With a heavy heart Barrow started to read it through.

Beatrice began her address to the Cadbury factory workers, in her capacity as a shareholder of the firm. She wanted to thank the workers, but also to offer them a heartfelt apology. Her gratitude was for the 'many privileges' she had enjoyed by virtue of her father's gift to her of company shares. But an apology was owed to them, the Cadbury employees, too, for up to now she had taken her legacy – which had come about by the fruits of *their* labour – for granted, entirely without thinking. For this she was deeply sorry.

But there was good news, she said. A fundamental change in society was coming and the capitalist order 'like all other evils' was 'preparing its own destruction'. Soon, she predicted, power would be transferred from 'a few individuals' to 'the large numbers of men and women who actually produce the income'. In preparation for the revolutionary change, she had decided (with her husband's willing co-operation) to take the lead, so that others might follow, and 'surrender voluntarily the exclusive right of possession' and share her legacy 'with the community at large.' Put simply, she was offering all her shares to be used by the Cadbury workers for the greater good of society.

The income from the shares could, she suggested, be used by a committee representing all workers, from the directors down to 'the most humble co-operators', for the good of society. This included work to 'combat starvation and disease, the repatriation of Siberian prisoners of war, better housing, relief of poverty, care for the sick, the aged, the oppressed...' and so it continued.

In a footnote to the document, Beatrice revealed how much money she had received from share dividends for the last two years. Following tax deductions, the amount was over three thousand pounds a year – at least twenty times the average yearly wage – and here she had frankly declared it for all the workers to see.

Barrow put the letter down. What on earth was he going to do about his little sister? He never knew what Beatrice and her husband would do next. Only a few months ago, she and Kees had been sentenced to a fortnight in prison for unlawfully preaching their anti-capitalist message in the streets of Utrecht. The judge had shown no leniency in spite of Beatrice being in the final stage of her pregnancy. Each night, Barrow and his wife Geraldine had knelt together in prayer asking for the safe arrival of the child. Candia had been born just two weeks after Beatrice's release.

No, he told himself, it was imperative to keep calm and think clearly. He would try and follow their late father's example of never seeming to judge or to disapprove. Barrow Cadbury was a natural peacemaker, with a reputation for being a reconciler of differences. However, although he strove to be gentle, he knew he could occasionally be impatient, or worse, when provoked. At work sometimes his temper flashed, a harsh word was uttered, to be followed quickly by a sincere and mortified apology.

As he said goodbye to Geraldine and left for work, he decided he would have to persuade Beatrice away from this insane proposal of hers. She must come to Birmingham immediately and talk to all of the family members on the board. Surely between them they would be able to make her see reason.

The weather that October had been mild and temperate but now, as he stepped outside briskly, it was as if the slight chill in the air presaged some of the difficulties that Beatrice's letter had already set in motion.

*

Neither Kees nor her children wanted her to go alone, but travelling together as a family was impossible. Since Kees's expulsion from England, he had been forbidden to enter Britain ever again so Betty had no choice but to go without her husband. Although she looked forward to seeing her brothers and sisters for the first time since her enforced relocation to Bilthoven, Betty also felt torn. She did not enjoy spending time apart from Kees. The girls surrounded their mother and pleaded with her to come back soon. They would be safely looked after by the family carer.

Kees and Betty walked hand-in-hand to Bilthoven train

station where they said an emotional farewell. Even before they parted Betty could not wait to be reunited with him. She knew she would miss the sight of his handsome face with its intense expression, always counterbalanced by the look of mischief in his eyes.

But Betty had a mission to complete. By the time she came back to Holland, she intended to be relieved of her Cadbury shares. The burden of guilt surrounding her legacy would finally be lifted. More importantly, she would be secure in the knowledge that the gift she had given would be used to support her and Kees's vision of a peaceful and more loving society. She stepped onto the train, and turned to wave goodbye.

Part I
The Early Years of Little B

1
A Never-ending Delight,
1884-1891

BEATRICE WAS STILL refusing to eat properly. Her nursemaid relayed this alarming news to the baby's mother, Emma Jane, who in turn anxiously told her husband Richard when he returned home from his long day's work at the Bournville factory. Their one-year-old daughter would only eat bread and butter, and take a drink of sweetened cocoa.

The trouble had begun as soon as Beatrice was weaned onto solid food. From an early age she knew her own mind and palate. She rejected any food with meat in it, no matter how well their cook tried to disguise it; she eschewed her feeding bottle and would only take drinks from a cup.

Her parents were in despair over their youngest child and Dr Carr, the family physician, was called in. To Emma Jane's alarm, he said that her precious baby was in danger of severe malnourishment and would more than likely end up with rickets if she continued to resist eating a more varied diet.

Trying to persuade Beatrice was a frustrating game that ended up involving the whole family. Her elder brothers and sisters tried to tempt her at mealtimes – with a piece of banana, or a succulent strawberry – but with limited success. Emma Jane, a keen proponent of alternative medicine, experimented with natural tonics in the hope it would build up her daughter's appetite. Beatrice's nursemaid resorted to feeding her Neave's Food Supplement, a specialist baby food with 'flesh and bone-forming constituents'.

In the meantime, Dr Carr advised cod liver oil and a massage of her limbs morning and night, as well as regular chest and back rubs.

Luckily for Beatrice, there was no shortage of money to buy the latest medical treatments, as well as a surplus of fresh wholesome food delivered daily to the family home. By an accident of birth, she had been born into one of Birmingham's wealthiest manufacturing families and, while there were no guarantees in matters of life and death, the odds of survival were stacked firmly in her favour. She was destined to flourish.

*

The last of Richard and Emma Jane Cadbury's children was born at the family home, Moseley Hall, at a time when Moseley was a small village located three miles south of Birmingham's industrialised centre. Beatrice Cadbury arrived at exactly 5 o'clock on a fine spring morning on 28th April, 1884. She weighed a respectable 4lb 2oz and had dark hair and eyes of startling dark blue, inherited from her mother. As soon as Emma Jane had recovered from the rigours of childbirth, the rest of her children crowded round to look at the new arrival. Emma Jane and Richard's young daughters, Edith, twelve, Helen, seven, and Margaret (Daisy), aged six, chattered excitedly as they bent over the crib. The older and grown-up siblings – the girls' half-brothers and half-sister – were just as pleased: Barrow, Jessie, William and Richard Junior smiled and laughed as they looked on.

Affluent parents took great pleasure in recording the details of their children's health and physical development in a Life Register, the Victorian equivalent of today's Baby Book. Beatrice's teeth came through early and were pronounced 'strong, white and regular'. Like her father, Richard, Beatrice was noticeably 'very good tempered'. However, a bout of whooping cough (although it would not be given that name for another twenty years) when Beatrice was four months old terrified them all. The whole family listened in agony to 'Little B' as she coughed and coughed for what seemed an eternity, each one willing her to draw in the life-saving breath through lips that had turned blue. But with swift medical attention she passed through the illness with no long-term effects and was otherwise healthy, apart from her spell of fussiness over food. Beatrice grew into a pretty child, with eyes of cornflower blue. Along with her 'good' teeth, she was blessed with a fine English rose complexion.

Her birth had marked the start of a golden period for the Cadbury family, where business success at the Bournville Works melded with a deeply satisfying family life.

Life had not always been so sweet for her parents.

*

Beatrice's mother, Emma Jane Wilson, was born on Christmas Day, 1846, in the Greet area of South East Birmingham. She was one of seven surviving children: ten in all were born to her parents, John Annis Wilson and Emma Wilson (née Smith). Although initially well-off, John Wilson's early investment in the railways had proved disastrous – to his shame, he lost a great deal of his fortune. Money was tight, therefore, and Mrs Wilson struggled to keep the household together financially. She was a formidable disciplinarian, whose Anglican faith imbued her with a strong sense of righteousness. Mrs Wilson's strictness was so fearsome that she terrified and upset the mother's help, a timid

Irish girl called Ann, whom Mrs Wilson employed in the house (sharing the costs with a neighbour). To Mrs Wilson's mind, Ann was dreadfully indulgent with the children. She would say to her in despair, 'I shall never be able to bring up my children well, while you are in the house.'

Mrs Wilson taught all the children herself and had dreams of starting her own school one day as a way to supplement the family's pitiful income. Lessons took place in a classroom at home. While Emma Jane, in particular, was an intelligent child and a keen scholar, her schooling was sacrificed to babysitting duties; she was often required to look after her baby brother, Willie.

Although strict, Mr and Mrs Wilson ran a happy home and when John Wilson died suddenly and unexpectedly in 1861, Mrs Wilson and the children were devastated. At just thirty-nine, Mrs Wilson was suddenly alone and without any savings to fall back on. No provision had been made for the children's further education, and it was only thanks to the financial help of a family friend (known as Aunt Richardson) that Emma Jane was sent at the age of nineteen to Switzerland, where she learned French and German to follow her plans of becoming a governess.

Meanwhile, to avoid destitution, Mrs Wilson had to find an income for herself and her other children. She had a number of short-term tutoring jobs, but nothing permanent. In 1869, it was her good fortune to meet a man called Mr Richard Cadbury shortly after he, too, had been widowed and left with four young children to look after. He found her a wonderfully sympathetic companion and a source of practical motherly advice on how to look after his distraught offspring. Eventually, he asked her if she would move into his house in Wheeleys Road in Edgbaston, Birmingham, to help care for his children.

Mrs Wilson was strongly impressed by her employer. Richard Cadbury was a businessman with a deep regard for the welfare of children. His walk home from the factory he owned took him through the poverty-stricken streets of Birmingham. He found the level of child deprivation and neglect he witnessed daily hard to tolerate; his throat would tighten with emotion. He told Mrs Wilson he wanted to do something to help the children whose mothers were out at work all day. Having been already struck by her nurturing attitude, he asked Mrs Wilson if she would run a children's day centre for him. Somewhat chuffed, she immediately wrote to Emma Jane in Switzerland to tell her about it.

This crèche in Bishopsgate Street was the first of its kind in England. Richard Cadbury would sometimes turn up at the end of the day to see the mothers collect their children, noting in his diary how pleased the women seemed to be 'to find their children so happy and with clean faces too, which is a blessing many of them were total strangers to before.'

And so, Richard Cadbury and Mrs Wilson found they were a good team. Neither of them imagined that two years later she would become his mother-in-law.

*

Richard Cadbury was born in 1835, the second eldest son of John Cadbury and his vivacious wife, Candia. John owned a shop in Bull Street in the middle of Birmingham. As a young man, John Cadbury had been sent by his father, Richard Tapper Cadbury, to learn about the commodities industry at its commercial centre in Mincing Lane, London. It was here, while on his City apprenticeship, that John Cadbury spotted a gap in the market for selling tea, coffee and other non-alcoholic beverages, including drinking cocoa. In 1824 he returned to Birmingham and opened his first premises. There was a strong moral dimension to John Cadbury's choice of trade. He was a member of The Society of Friends, known colloquially as the Quakers, and they played a key part in the Temperance Movement drive to provide the working classes with an alternative to drinking alcohol. When John opened his tea shop, therefore, he was satisfying both his entrepreneurial ambitions and his Quaker conscience.

In 1847, owing to the building of a new railway line, John was forced to move premises but by now he was more interested in manufacturing cocoa products, so he moved to a factory in Bridge Street and began to concentrate more on making drinking chocolate.

Richard Cadbury's childhood was idyllic but when he reached adulthood he was expected to join the family business, which he did in 1850. In 1855, his mother, Candia, died of consumption and his father, John, never quite recovered his spirit. His appetite for the world of commerce waned and his body was ravaged by arthritis. This, followed by a downturn in the demand for drinking chocolate and chocolate blocks, meant that by 1861, the business was struggling. Richard and his younger brother George felt morally obliged to take over their father's ailing business and so later that year they formed Cadbury Brothers to try and turn the company around. When their mother died, she had left Richard and George the sum of four thousand pounds each. They resolved they would do one thing: plough their inheritance back into the family business to restore its flagging fortunes. To the outside world, the brothers, aged twenty-five and twenty-one, spoke in noble terms of the privilege of having their 'integrity of purpose' tested. Between themselves however, they could not hide the terror of the abyss they were staring into. Bankruptcy was a disgrace within Quaker circles and they felt themselves hanging perilously close to this shame.

The immense pressure Richard was under that year was alleviated somewhat by his marriage to Elizabeth Adlington. She was a schoolfriend of his sister Maria, and her father William Adlington was a well-known and respected Quaker from Mansfield. It was a good match. Elizabeth was intelligent, well-educated and a skilled seamstress; she had been thoroughly prepared for marriage. Following their wedding they moved into 17 Wheeleys Road, situated within the sound of the bells of

Edgbaston Church.

During the next three years Cadbury Brothers hovered on the brink of failure. As the months went by Richard saw his mother's legacy dwindle terrifyingly to four hundred pounds. The two brothers had considerable business acumen between them, but the company was stuck in a quagmire. The accounts books of 1861, 1862 and 1863 showed considerable losses and by early 1864 the brothers were contemplating leaving the business for alternative careers. Over tea one day they discussed what they might do. Richard liked the idea of becoming a land surveyor and George saw himself as a tea planter in the Himalayas. Richard began totting up their assets in preparation for selling the business.

When it came to it though, their faith in God and their refusal to give in won out. Their hard patience, persistence and sheer grit had its reward. In 1864 the accounts showed a small profit. Although it was minuscule, this was just the spur the Cadbury brothers needed to renew their confidence in the business. They had turned the corner.

Richard and George were hands-on employers, the superintendents of everything in the company, and that included the welfare of their employees. The factory opened at six and the brothers provided free coffee and buns for the men, and milk with buns for the women. (Coffee was considered a little too stimulating for female workers.) The brothers cut their own expenses down to the bone – foregoing a daily newspaper and existing on a supper of bread and butter as they stayed at the Bridge Street factory long into the night.

They also introduced incentives to encourage good employee behaviour, including small bonuses for turning up to work on time. Another initiative was The Pledge – a promise made by employees to resist the temptation to eat chocolate on the production line. Again, a financial incentive was attached.

For Richard, family life intertwined with business. In

September, 1862, Elizabeth gave birth to Barrow Cadbury. A girl named Alice was born in 1864, who passed away at seven months. In 1865, Jessie, another girl, was born and in 1867 William Adlington came along.

At the end of 1868, a third son, Richard, arrived but along with his birth came tragedy. Elizabeth's health had been failing for a long time. One of Richard Senior's most sorrowful moments during the lean times of Cadbury had been when he took his wife and children on a rare family outing to Pebble Mill. When Elizabeth was taken ill he did not have enough money to catch a cab home.

The strain of giving birth proved too much for Elizabeth in her weakened state. Just ten days after Richard Junior was born, Elizabeth passed away on New Year's Eve, leaving behind a broken-hearted Richard and four young children: seven-year-old Barrow, Jessie, almost four, William, not quite two, and baby Richard. They woke on the first day of 1869 to find their mother gone.

*

Mrs Wilson wrote to Emma Jane in Switzerland from the Cadbury household to say the crèche that Mr Cadbury had started was going well. Furthermore, his four bewildered children were slowly coming to terms with life without their mother and she had done her best to comfort and support them.

In 1870, Emma Jane was due to return to England, having finished her training. She hoped her fluency in French and German would make her employable, but where to live in the meantime? Mrs Wilson asked her employer if Emma Jane could move into the house until suitable accommodation arrangements could be made. Richard Cadbury, generous to a fault, said of course.

It was a crisp autumn morning when Emma Jane journeyed to Wheeleys Road. She was nervous as she rang the doorbell, wondering if she really *was* as welcome in the household as her mother had suggested. At that moment, Richard Cadbury happened to be passing through the hallway and he opened the door himself. It seemed like fate.

She registered a kindly smile, with hazel eyes etched with woe and anxiety. He, in turn, felt moved by the sight of this vivacious young creature with dark blue eyes on his doorstep. As he welcomed her inside, an instant mutual attraction sprang up between them.

A month later they announced their engagement.

*

Although they each came from religiously devout backgrounds, there were differences. Emma Jane was a member of the congregational church at Carrs Lane; Richard was a Quaker. Strictly speaking, Quakers were not supposed to marry outside the Society of Friends. The thinking behind this rule was that Quaker beliefs should not be 'diluted'. There was also an age difference. She was twenty-three; he was thirty-five. But they had things in common, too. They both loved Switzerland and he had a longing to travel more, which she shared. She had a refreshingly broad outlook on life for the era: she was intelligent and open-minded (for example, she was strongly committed to the use of homeopathic medicine). She was exciting, almost *avant-garde*.

In October, they announced their intention to marry with some nervousness. 'I have told my brothers and sister today,' Richard wrote in a letter to Emma Jane, 'and they are perfectly satisfied with the step I have taken.' He was relieved that he had the approval of his brothers, especially George, and his sister, Maria.

Support was more enthusiastic from Mrs Wilson, who, Richard noted, 'seems not only satisfied, but really happy at the thought that we love one another as we do.'

With a regard for propriety, Richard moved out of his home in Wheeleys Road before his marriage and letters went back and forth daily, sometimes twice a day, between the couple. Emma Jane's letters appear not to have survived, but she later admitted to being daunted by the responsibilities that lay ahead of her. She had the difficult task of bonding with her four step-children and although Richard assured her that Barrow and Jessie were 'delighted' with the French dolls she had given them (souvenirs brought back from Switzerland) at twenty-three she felt ill-prepared for a ready-made family.

Richard was a prolific and expressive letter-writer. He could also be coy, once comparing Emma Jane to a nurse in one of his children's picture books. 'I do not mean in likeness,' he wrote, 'but in mind, for you would be such a loving nurse. It would almost be worthwhile to be ill to have your loving face near ...' These notes, composed while he was at work, hint at his sexual desire as well as his craving for female warmth and companionship.

On Valentines Day, 1871, scores of cards arrived in the post for the women at the Bridge Street factory, but Richard kept these missives in the office until the end of the day to avoid over-excitement. Although Richard was a strict moral guardian, he was secretly in as much thrall to love as the exuberant factory girls.

That same February, Barrow was sent away to boarding school. At eight years old, it was time for him to be a big boy but even so, as Richard noted to Emma Jane, his son's lips 'quivered a little as he said goodbye'.

Emma Jane married Richard on 25th July, 1871, less than a year after they had met. The marriage took place at an Anglican church in Bristol. Aunt Richardson, who had paid for Emma Jane's schooling in Switzerland, held the wedding party at her house. Those attending included Richard's younger unmarried brothers, George and Henry Cadbury. John Cadbury, Emma Jane's father-in-law, was unable to be there because of ill health, but on the way to their honeymoon the wedding couple stopped off at his home where he presented them with just-picked grapes from his hothouse and gave Emma Jane a little purse full of gold.

For two years Emma Jane resisted joining the Society of Friends. Richard went to his Quaker meetings, accompanied by Emma Jane; likewise he visited her church just as regularly. To Emma, the Quaker meeting was a strange, barely comprehensible affair. It took place every Sunday at the Quaker Meeting House in Bull Street, right in the centre of Birmingham. The men and women sat on opposite sides of the high-ceilinged room, each on long pews made of real oak. There was nothing for the eye to catch in these austere surroundings – no religious iconography or other shows of faith. Hardest of all for the music-loving Emma Jane was the absence of hymn-singing during the worship, and the long periods of silence that seemed interminable.

Despite these reservations, in 1873 Emma Jane announced that she was ready to join her husband in the Society. Her youngest brother, Willie, also became a Friend.

Marriage agreed with Richard and Emma Jane. Their first child together was Edith, born in 1872. Then came two more girls: Helen in 1877, and the following year, Margaret (always known as Daisy). Family life was happy and the business was on the up, too.

*

Much had happened since the turning point in the mid-1860s when the fortunes of Cadbury Brothers had changed for the better. The business stabilised, then began to grow, and the brothers introduced advertising, which enabled them to position cocoa effectively as a health drink. Its pure and wholesome goodness became a unique selling point in an era where food adulteration was rife. Richard, a supremely talented artist, began to concentrate on packaging, and was inspired by trips to Switzerland where he delighted in the scenes of the countryside and the invigorating image they conjured up. He was creative in his approach, even using his own daughter, Jessie, in some of the early product designs of Cadbury Brothers.

By the late 1870s, the Bridge Street factory was becoming too small to cope with the increased demand. Richard and George began to conceive of building a larger, more modern factory on the outskirts of Birmingham. It would be to everyone's benefit, George said, if the factory were located on a green field site, not least of all the employees who would benefit from a clean environment. Richard, who shared the same obsession with clean air, was only too willing to agree. They found a site of fifteen acres, approximately four miles outside Birmingham with excellent road, rail and canal links.

George sketched out a plan for the new factory. The original blueprint showed the different departments and manufacturing areas. From an early stage provision was made for the welfare of the workers. The plans included a dressing room, where employees could change their clothes at the start of their shift and leave their wet shoes in a specially-heated drying area. There was also a large dining room that would serve nutritious cooked meals daily.

The new factory was going to be called Bournbrook, in honour of the River Bourn whose crystal clear waters flowed through the site.

The transition from Bridge Street to the new site was scheduled to take place over the summer of 1879. All went smoothly and in September the workers arrived at their new premises to begin production. They were surprised and delighted by the ground-breaking staff facilities inside the building, and the Cadbury brothers had further surprises in store outside. Next to the factory, a cricket pitch and a football field had been built for the men, while a play area with swings and wooden benches made an ideal place for the ladies to relax during breaks and lunch-times. Richard and George wanted the workplace to be comfortable and refreshing to the soul and senses.

The plans for the Works had been meticulously carried out and only one aspect had been wrong: the name.

Unsatisfied with the original, Bournbrook, Richard and George decided to add the French-sounding suffix, -ville, in order to conjure up an air of sophistication. And so the new Works was finally complete. Bournville.

The Bournville Works was a roaring success. Within four years, business turnover had doubled. A journalist from the *Midland Echo* was stunned by what he saw during an extensive visit to the factory in 1884. First, there was the lush green setting and then, inside – 'one hesitates to call it a factory'. To him, the factory was reminiscent of a 'high class school'. He could have been in South Kensington, rather than Birmingham.

> 'Once in the presence of the principals,' [the newspaper reporter gushed] 'the term "factory" seems even more distasteful, for although undoubtedly keen businessmen, their appearance, manners and conversation have so little suggestive of the typical factory owner about them, and so many implications of benevolence and kindly feeling that one becomes irresistibly impressed with the thought that money for themselves was the last thing on their minds ... These men regard those in their employ not as part of the machinery, but as human beings for whose well-being they are in large measure responsible.'

*

1884 was significant in many ways. At the start of the year, Richard was wealthy enough to be able to move his family to a brand new home, Moseley Hall, in the Moseley district of Birmingham. It was here that Beatrice's birth would take place, marking the start of a magical period in which the commercial success of Cadbury intensified the pleasures of family life.

Moseley Hall was a wonderful place for Richard and Emma

Jane's youngest child to grow up. The former home of J. B. Priestley, it was a large and rambling mansion, with long passages, high ceilings and plenty of cupboards and attic rooms for playing hide-and-seek. (Forward-thinking Emma Jane had designated one of the rooms in the attic as a Screaming Room where the children could let off steam as noisily as they liked.) Outside, the surrounding grounds were vast, with a walled kitchen garden and a fig tree that bore plenty of luscious fruit in the summer.

Through the windows of the drawing room another tree could be seen – a Copper beech that bore a more unusual fruit at Easter. Every Good Friday morning the children would wake to find that the tree had sprouted hot cross buns during the night.

The grounds surrounding the hall included a bluebell wood and the garden teemed with so many rabbits it was soon nicknamed 'The Bunny House'. It was a fairytale home, and made all the sweeter by the addition of two family dogs: Duke, a retriever and Barry, a St Bernard puppy whom Beatrice adored. For her fourth birthday she was bought her very own Shetland pony, Dolly. Up until then she had ridden her nursery rocking horse, Dapple Grey, but her excitement knew no bounds when she sat upon Dolly's back and paraded proudly around the grounds, led carefully along by her nursemaid, Emma Denham.

Weekdays at Moseley Hall began with the assembly of the family at 7.30am. Richard and Emma Jane, the children from his first marriage – Barrow, Jessie, William and Richard, all now adults – and the four girls, Edith, Helen, Daisy and Beatrice, would all join together for breakfast. Another frequent guest was Polly, a sociable and sweet-toothed parrot from Brazil, who liked to perch on Beatrice's shoulder and take milk and sugar from her hand.

There would be a bible reading and a prayer, 'committing the whole household to God's care and guidance during the coming day', before Richard Cadbury kissed each of his children and his wife then set off for the Bournville Works. He caught a lift with the letter van, the vehicle he called his 'chariot'. This was just one example of the contradictory mixture of opulence and austerity that co-existed in the Cadbury household at the time. When he arrived at work, Richard or his brother, George, would hold a short service with a passage from scripture for the Bournville workers.

Beatrice had her own routines. Her mother considered cold baths to be beneficial, so every morning Beatrice endured a bracing wash in the bathtub, with her much-loved nursemaid ready to whisk her out as soon as she could, complaining that Beatrice's lips were turning blue. Emma Jane had picked up many influences from her time in Switzerland and one of these was the belief that hot baths were an unnecessary indulgence. She continued to have her own way in these domestic matters.

*

As Richard became richer so grew the challenge of reconciling his personal wealth with his Quaker beliefs. Both Richard and George saw themselves as guardians or custodians of wealth, and with the privilege of their blessed fortune came the responsibility to help others through 'good works'. As well as Richard's commitment to the Gospel Temperance Mission, the cause most dear to him was the Adult School Movement. He ran a men's bible and literacy class, which met in Highgate every Sunday at 7.30am. He was a patient and extremely diligent teacher who hated to miss a class and in winter time he would walk through deep snow in order not to let his men down. When Beatrice was born, Emma Jane became involved with an equivalent women's group at Highgate, called the Mother's Meeting.

Beatrice's parents took their civic duties seriously and the children were expected to do their bit, too, to help the less fortunate. In late spring, Beatrice and her nursemaid would pick bluebells from the field at Moseley Hall to make posies to distribute in the poorer areas of Birmingham. Emma Jane encouraged the girls to hold pin sales at home, with the 'proceeds' going to help underprivileged children. At Christmas time, the sisters would form their own mini-production line, grating suet, stoning raisins and washing currants to make Christmas puddings for families in need.

The contributions expected from the Cadbury girls increased when Richard began organising the first of the day trips to Moseley Hall for the children of the Birmingham slums. When Richard saw the children arrive they were a ragged bunch, with matted unwashed hair; many had no shoes or boots, nor coats or scarves to protect their fragile bodies from the elements. Most were undernourished. The contrast for Richard between these groups and his own happy healthy children was almost too much to bear.

"Go upstairs and raid your cupboards," he would say to his girls, his emotions making him sound brusque. "You have plenty. They have nothing." To Beatrice, there would be tough choices to make as she clambered up the staircase to the nursery. In her toy cupboard there was the usual jumble of storybooks, dolls, bears and painting equipment. Meanwhile, Richard would be in the kitchen ordering Cook to make a vat of hot milk to which he would add cocoa, stirring it with a stick. Helen and Daisy would be commandeered to serve cocoa and a bun to each of the children on the lawn outside.

As a girl Beatrice was intensely curious about these children. Where did they live? Did they go to school? And why were they so dirty? There were subtle indications to Beatrice that a very different world existed beyond the privileged confines of Moseley Hall. Even from a tender age she was becoming aware that there were others less fortunate, and that this fact troubled Daddy.

*

By the time Beatrice was seven, a new and very modern kindergarten had opened next door to Edgbaston High School, the school her elder sisters attended and where Beatrice would later go. The kindergarten was run according to the Fröebel method – established by the German-born pioneer of children's education, Freidrich Fröebel – and it provided an educational experience that was rare in Victorian Britain, being both child-centred and experiential, with an emphasis on learning through play. Modern Emma Jane persuaded Richard that it would be ideal for Beatrice: it was relatively close by and there was even a small farm at the back of the kindergarten which Beatrice, with her fondness for animals, would be sure to love.

All the children adored Moseley Hall, none more so than Beatrice, but their parents were thinking of moving. Richard had secretly harboured the dream of a new home built solely to his own specifications. Unbeknown to their children, Richard and Emma Jane had been wondering for some time about donating Moseley Hall for use as a convalescent home.

The couple were concerned about the slow recovery times for sick children at the children's hospital and they wanted to create an environment away from the industrialised centre of Birmingham. They had been looking for suitable premises on which to build a convalescent centre – ideally with fresh air and pleasant country surroundings – before they realised that they should be looking at what they already had. Why not Moseley Hall itself? After all, the lease was coming to an end and thus they would be free to build the house of their dreams with an entirely clear conscience.

With excess funds from a phenomenally successful business, Richard could afford to create his ideal home. He bought some land not far from Moseley Hall, set on a hilltop with sloping lawns. The front of the house would be at Queensbridge Road and adjacent to Highbury, the home of Joseph Chamberlain. A gifted artist, Richard spent months designing every last detail before handing over his plans to the architect, William Alexander. The new house would be called Uffculme, a name that derived from the village in Devon where the Cadbury ancestors came from.

On the day that Uffculme was completed and Moseley Hall was officially handed over, one of the ministers at the ceremony recalled Richard's excitement: "It was so like him, yet I never saw him so humble or joyous."

In November, 1891, the family moved in to their new home. Although there had been many visits to Uffculme while it was being built, it was still a wrench for seven-year-old Beatrice to leave the Bunny House and the bluebell wood behind. She was dismayed by the new house and she cried. The familiar cosiness of Moseley Hall had gone and the mature gardens she so loved were replaced by empty lawns with newly-planted trees.

Richard had created a house fit for a successful entrepreneur. For the first time ever he had allowed himself to have fun with his money and if there was the slightest element of showing off, perhaps he had earned that privilege. Certainly, the Quaker tenet of simplicity was nowhere to be found.

On entering Uffculme, visitors were greeted by a vast hall containing a magnificent fireplace with two chairs on either side and a grand staircase leading off it, up to the first floor. Mounted all along the walls of the hall were stuffed birds and butterflies trapped behind glass. Beatrice hated it. Even Barrow thought it was like some dreadful museum. Artefacts from Richard's travels adorned every available space. There was even room for an organ which Edith, the most accomplished organist in the family, could play.

Perhaps the only saving grace was the light that came through to the hall on one side from the double-height conservatory, which itself was furnished with ten-foot high palms, and held treasures for Beatrice such as a white cockatoo called 'Cockey Boy' and dear little goldfish swimming in a pool.

After the upheaval of the move, family life settled down again and Richard found a renewed devotion to mission work. The planning and care that had gone into building the Bournville Works was now channelled into Uffculme. The informal gatherings for the underprivileged that Beatrice had witnessed at Moseley Hall continued on a more ambitious scale. Open tea sheds were built in the grounds of Uffculme so that they could be used all year round to prepare lunches and afternoon teas. Later, there would be a gymnasium and a tennis court, to be opened occasionally for public use.

For Beatrice it was an untroubled childhood with complete freedom from want; a never-ending delight of comfort and privilege. Yet even by the age of seven she was aware of standing out, like gold thread running through sacking – she was a 'have' in a world of 'have-nots'.

And she, like her father, would have to find a way to reconcile that.

2

Death of a Father, Rebirth of Cadbury, 1891-1899

THE GOLDEN PERIOD which had begun with Beatrice's birth in 1884 continued well into the next decade. Richard and Emma Jane's young family was growing and maturing and the couple watched with pleasure as their children developed and flourished.

Meanwhile, the factory at Bournville continued to be spectacularly profitable – by 1890 the Cadbury brothers had managed to quadruple the sales of ten years previously. The Works was now employing almost a thousand workers. Their bestselling product was still Cocoa Essence, lauded for its pure and wholesome ingredients, but other packaging innovations included beautiful Fancy Gift-Boxes.

Although he was still very busy with factory life, Richard began to allow himself periods of travel. He often dashed over to France to see his sister, Beatrice's Auntie Maria, who had made her life there after previously being tied to the home looking after their father John Cadbury until his death in 1889. During one of these visits to Boulogne, in 1892, Richard wrote to Beatrice:

'We are so glad to have thy sweet little notes that come over the sea to us ... Dearest love from mother and thy loving daddy.' For the Cadburys, holidays were an essential refreshment, a break from the life of running the factory and a chance to learn more about the world in which they lived. Richard was keen to explore new areas and he enjoyed the opportunities for learning that travel presented. As well as educating himself, he loved passing that knowledge on to others, especially members of his Adult School class.

In spite of the lavish lifestyle, Quakerism still remained central to Richard Cadbury's life. He had a literal belief in the teaching of the bible and the Quaker influence manifested itself in many ways. Alcohol and gambling were forbidden, of course, but so were other 'worldly pleasures' such as concert performances, stage plays and the opera. All of these were considered unacceptable pastimes (although, at home, Emma Jane played the piano, which Richard enjoyed). Beatrice felt the first effects of her father's somewhat stern moral influence when she turned eleven and changed schools.

*

After four years of child-centred schooling at the Fröebel kindergarten (for this she had her mother to thank) it was time for Beatrice to undergo a more formal education. Beatrice began her secondary schooling in 1895 at Edgbaston High School for Girls on the Hagley Road in Birmingham. Edgbaston High School had been established by various distinguished local families, of Quaker and Unitarian traditions, who wanted a liberal and well-rounded education for their daughters. Richard Cadbury felt he could rest assured that the rules his family lived by at home would be reflected in the school room.

When eleven-year-old Beatrice set off for school one day in September she was following in the footsteps of her elders. Jessie, her half-sister, had attended the school, as had Geraldine, Barrow's new wife. The first day would be less of an ordeal as her sister Helen, seven years older, was in her final year at the school (and newly-appointed Head Girl) and would be on hand to reassure Beatrice as she settled in. The two girls made their journey in the family's horse-drawn carriage, the hooves clip-clopping along the Hagley Road.

Pupils at Edgbaston High School were not required to wear a school uniform as such, merely a school tie and a hatband to signify the school identity. Girls were therefore free to wear what they liked – within reason. The standard form of dress expected was a high-necked blouse, with a petersham belt, tucked into a long skirt, which came just above the ankle. Beatrice noticed that some of the more daring girls wore a range of combs in their hair too, leading the teachers to complain of too much frivolity. But there was no danger of sartorial excess in the Cadbury children.

Beatrice took as full a part in school life as was possible for a girl whose father severely disapproved of certain activities. Times had now changed in the school and a new tradition had developed of the girls putting on a play at Christmas time – one in the upper school and one in the lower, with one production usually performed in French or German. But in the Cadbury household, at least as far as Richard was concerned, acting was considered to have an air of licentiousness about it, and Beatrice was excluded from taking part or even attending the final show. At this stage in her life she did not dream of questioning her parents' authority. They knew best, but even so she felt a pang of longing as she stood on the sidelines missing the excitement and thrill of the preparations.

Being cold was a constant complaint amongst the girls, and Beatrice, in spite of her daily cold bath, was not inured to it either. The classrooms at Edgbaston High School were heated by a real fire with a guard, which provided adequate heat for the mistresses to warm themselves by, while they opened the classroom windows wide to encourage ventilation – and never mind if the girls froze. Despite the crude attempt at ventilation this did not stop outbreaks of disease – scarlet fever, mumps and once, alarmingly, an outbreak of smallpox – but Beatrice managed to avoid these. Minor inconveniences, such as chilblains, were a regular hazard.

Beatrice continued to travel with her sister in that first year, either by carriage or seated back-to-back in the family dogcart, rather than taking the Moseley (school) Bus. She missed out on the fun of travelling with the other pupils on the bus, where the behaviour – even amongst these genteel young ladies – could be riotous. Not for Beatrice the drama of desperately completing homework on the bus, or the shrieks and giggles as the girls waved at men driving by in open motor cars. There were some hair-raising tales, including the bus being late because of a pencil case thrown overboard as a delaying tactic to enable the previous night's homework to be finished. For Beatrice, there was always a feeling of being on the outside, on the edges of all the fun.

Edgbaston High School had a progressive educational system with a broad curriculum that was both highly academic and yet inclusive of extra-curricular activities. The previous headmistress, Miss Cooper, had been enthusiastic, inspiring and determined to stamp her mark on the school. Described as 'a real bluestocking' she had a Cambridge certificate and was keen that her girls should have high aspirations for themselves.

Miss Cooper had instilled a hardworking ethos in her charges, which led a school inspector to describe the educational provision at Edgbaston High School as 'not only satisfactory but, in some respects, altogether surprising. I was unprepared for so much general excellence, or ... the thorough mastery by so many girls of so large a number of subjects.' The same inspector also praised 'the ladylike tone and bearing of the school', the 'frank respectfulness' of the girls towards their teachers and their 'healthy freedom from silliness, tittering and affectation'. Miss Cooper viewed good examination results as a ticket to any career her pupils might wish to enter (although, at the same time, she lamented the tendency of academic examinations to distort and narrow the curriculum). She passionately argued the benefits of a broad-based curriculum. "You are ... not merely a purchaser at a knowledge shop," she would frequently remind the girls.

To Beatrice's surprise and delight, sport and exercise featured in school life. Under headmistress Miss Japp's reign at Edgbaston High School between 1895 and 1899 – which coincided with Beatrice's time there – hockey was introduced, which Beatrice discovered she had a flair for and kept up for many years of her schooling. For all gym lessons the girls wore a navy-blue box-pleated tunic with a velvet yoke – which had a tendency to bulge unflatteringly, according to the more image-conscious girls – and a white flannel blouse underneath.

A growing body of opinion had rejected the idea that girls were feeble and interested in only timid pursuits. This was a real move away from the traditional Victorian values of grace and posture, of training the body, with walking and riding being the only acceptable forms of exercise for young ladies. Instead, girls were able to indulge in more rough-and-tumble pursuits. In this respect, the school was very much ahead of its time, although this trend was not without its critics. The Cricket Club, for example, was somewhat controversial. The local press tut-tutted at the immodesty of young girls playing cricket, fearing it would create 'muscular maidens' whose chances of marriage would be forever blighted. Tennis, badminton and rounders were also added to Physical Education lessons. Calisthenics, a form of gymnastics, was taught to help the girls develop strong, supple bodies.

Pupils were also encouraged to contribute to a Garden Club and to the school magazine. While Beatrice's older sister, Helen, had been at the school she had created her own club, to 'win the souls of girls to Christ'. To qualify for membership, girls had to promise to carry round with them a pocket-sized version of the

New Testament (provided by Richard) and to read a portion of the bible every day. They called themselves The Pocket Testament League.

The school day began with registration and play from 9.15 to 9.30, followed by three 40-minute lectures, a ten-minute break for buns and milk, followed by two more 40-minute lectures before lunch. The school day ended at one o'clock.

Some girls proved to be high achievers – gaining entry to Oxbridge. Others, including Helen Cadbury, went to university colleges. Some Old Girls of Edgbaston High School entered teaching, medicine, and even forged careers in literature and art. Inevitably, some girls left school and then lived at home until they married but even then the school encouraged them to keep up with their studies and to ensure their minds stayed active through mental stimulation.

Beatrice got off to a flying start academically. Her first school report was something for her parents to be proud of. In the winter of 1895 her test results placed her in the top quarter of the class, and her report described her as 'a diligent, intelligent pupil', with a good memory ('spelling: excellent') as well as possessing a very good knowledge of the New Testament. She was commended for voluntarily learning bible verses each week by heart. Her best subject was French, perhaps not surprisingly given her mother's fluency in the language, and her weakest arithmetic. She also came top of the class in History and Geography. Richard and Emma Jane were delighted with the progress of their Little B.

But no sooner had Beatrice settled into her studies than the following term would prove to be full of distractions.

*

The previous year Richard and his brother, George, had jointly bought a holiday home at Wynd's Point in Malvern. It had been owned by Jenny Lind, the popular Swedish singer, who had died and was buried in Malvern Cemetery.

It soon became a tradition that each spring the Cadbury family would decamp to the house for three or four weeks at a stretch. Richard was in his element striding up the hilltops of Malvern, where he would stand with his coat open wide and arms spread out, declaring, "There's no air anywhere like Malvern air!"

In the spring of 1896 the family was due to go again and Beatrice was taken out of school for this trip. Malvern was a real treat. Before breakfast she would be up early to run up to the nearby fountain at St Ann's well to drink its cold and pure Malvern water. At other times, the family would cycle to Tewkesbury for breakfast in the hotel near to the Abbey. Beatrice enjoyed the clear days best when it was possible to see the spires of all three cathedrals at Gloucester, Hereford and Worcester from the hilltop.

Back at Wynd's Point, Richard and Emma Jane would entertain friends, including the likes of George Bernard Shaw and Ramsay MacDonald, who would become the first Labour Prime Minister in Britain in 1924. As Beatrice sat at the dinner table she would tune in and out of the grown-ups' conversations, catching fragments to do with the plight of the common man, and the Trafalgar Riots of 1886. Although perhaps not aware of it at the time, these discussions must have helped to add to the unease she had first experienced at the children's tea parties in Moseley Hall and Uffculme. But all too soon it was time to go – somewhat reluctantly – back home.

At the end of the spring term, Beatrice's second school report was not quite as glowing as the previous one had been. It recorded that she had missed 26 days in total. The headmistress, Miss Japp, wrote: 'Beatrice works very well but her progress has been hindered by absence this term'. Richard and Emma Jane, although devoted parents, had thought nothing of taking Beatrice away for the Malvern break. She was a bright girl, they reasoned, and surely a few days out of school could not do much harm. The

Head, however, was annoyed at this apparently cavalier attitude to their daughter's school attendance.

In truth, Beatrice's schooling had to compete with family activities throughout the whole of 1896 and the various excitements diverted her attention away from studying. In April, Beatrice's half-sister, Jessie, got married to Revd. T. G. Clarke and they went to live in Corby. Beatrice was bridesmaid and the whole family was caught up in the pre-wedding excitement. Then, on 25th July that year, Richard and Emma Jane were due to mark their 25th wedding anniversary.

First, there was to be a celebration where many of the Bournville workers came to a party held on the sloping lawns of the Uffculme estate. Two days later, another more intimate party was held for Quaker friends and relatives. The actual anniversary on 25th July was spent with nine hundred or so members of Richard's Adult School class, whom he was dearly fond of.

The children persuaded their parents that they should go away for a second honeymoon. Richard was reluctant to miss his Sunday morning Adult School class that weekend so they agreed on a short break in Malvern. In secret, Beatrice and her sisters decorated the open landau (a four-wheeled carriage) with flowers and also threaded foliage through the reins of the horses. An old shoe was tied to the back of the carriage for the departing couple.

In Beatrice's mind, her parents' love for each other was an inspiration, a 'radiant and beautiful example', as she would later describe it. In the anniversary photographs, Emma Jane was indeed beautiful, dressed in a full-length brocaded gown, with puffed sleeves, her waist still tiny after twenty-five years of marriage. At sixty-one, Richard was by now silver-haired, and his beard snow white, but he was still energetic. They remained two love-birds, devoted to each other and immensely proud of their children.

*

Richard had become almost addicted to travelling and his enthusiasm for holidays was contagious. To Beatrice, her daddy was like a child let out of school in the lead up to the trips.

Excursions were made to Colwyn Bay in Wales, climbing the Cader Idris with its glacial bowl, trying not to get caught in the mist. A summer holiday was spent on the coast of Ireland. On the beach Beatrice and her sisters were taken out to sea in a bathing machine – a Victorian contraption pulled by horses, which allowed the swimmers to get changed discreetly into swimwear before being deposited directly into the water, thus protecting them from prurient glances. When the girls had finished splashing in the water, they would be picked up and returned fully dressed once more onto the shoreline ready to stroll along the beach or build sandcastles.

Cornwall was another holiday favourite where, in Lizard, the children made their own adventures, exploring the rock pools and playing pirates at the Jolly Jenny, before returning for lunch or Beatrice's favourite treat: a scone with jam and thick Cornish cream. After lunch, Emma Jane would order Beatrice to have a little nap and then it would be time to go exploring again. The rhythm of the holidays was always the same: day-long excursions combined with lazy days spent roaming, with fresh air and plentiful amounts of wholesome food. No wonder the children were reluctant to go back to their studies.

Soon, European adventures beckoned with trips to France, Switzerland and Italy. Richard and Emma Jane were very proud of their girls, and took pride in the sight they made when they travelled as a party. On a family tour of Switzerland, where Jessie had accompanied them, Richard was delighted by the nickname he was given, 'The gentleman travelling with six ladies'.

The trips were of great educational value. In Pompeii they witnessed the excavation work being conducted, following the many volcano eruptions at Mount Vesuvius. (Beatrice was particularly excited by watching a coin being pressed into the glowing fluid lava.) Richard wrote to his son Richard Junior, who was in South Africa beginning his career as a fruit farmer: 'We saw in Milan the original picture of [sic] Leonardo da Vinci, The Last Supper'. He was similarly inspired by Rome with all its treasures, and by the works of the 'great men' of Florence: Michelangelo, Dante, Savonarola, Galileo. Richard's fascination was infectious and, through her father's eyes, Beatrice learned to see the glories of the world, of nature and botany, artistic wonders, and glimpses into the history of past ages. To experience these splendours first-hand was real learning, and to have it all explained by 'dearest daddy' instead of poring over a dry old textbook in the classroom, was just marvellous.

Beatrice's Head Teacher thought otherwise. Whilst Miss Japp would not have dared to criticise Emma Jane and Richard Cadbury openly, a rebuke to them could nevertheless be detected in Beatrice's school reports that year. Unsurprisingly, by the end of 1896, Beatrice had shown a marked dip in her test grades and she had slid towards the bottom third of the class.

She had no need to worry about that. She loved and trusted her parents to do what was best, and Daddy worked so hard at the factory that it was wonderful to see him relaxing.

*

But trouble was brewing inside the Cadbury household. Underneath the surface of their apparently idyllic family life, two of the daughters were quietly rebelling against their upbringing. Richard and Emma Jane had been relieved to see Jessie and then Edith married and now launched in life, but Helen and Daisy, the next two eldest girls, began to challenge the moral and religious constraints imposed by their parents.

After leaving Edgbaston High School and The Mount School in Yorkshire, Helen had gone to London to study at Westfield College. Up until that point she had accepted her parents' Quaker beliefs and indeed had embraced them enthusiastically as a young teenager, not only in her school gang, The Pocket Testament League, but also by helping Richard during his temperance mission work. She had been a loyal ally to the cause.

But in London she was exposed to new and more sophisticated influences and realised – initially with some regret – that her parents' literal interpretation of the bible and its teaching was simplistic and somewhat naïve. Her discussions with her tutor, Miss Robertson, left her unsettled, confused even. There was no question that Miss Robertson was of good moral character, and yet she had a different approach to scripture.

Helen gradually turned away from Quakerism; she stopped going to the weekly Quaker Meeting, and began, tentatively, to explore the forbidden 'worldly pleasures' of musical concerts and opera. As part of her studies she went to Germany to study music in Dresden. Her father wrote letters from home to ask if she was still 'winning friends to Christ' as she had once done as a schoolgirl. But Helen was no longer interested in this pious pursuit. If anything, she now felt embarrassed by her childhood enterprise.

However, being instilled with a good conscience and a scruple against openly defying her mother and father, she still wanted their blessing on her decision to go to the opera. She wrote to ask permission and Richard wrote back to say, 'If you feel you must go, then go,' but (he urged her), 'Make it a matter of earnest prayer, and God will guide you aright.'

Helen was somewhat disarmed by this calm response, perhaps hoping for an outright ban against which she could then justifiably rebel. However, she opted to pursue her interest in the opera and, having made that decision, her attitude to her faith cooled even further.

Daisy, only 18 months younger than Helen, was going through the same inner conflict. Daisy was a lively and sporty girl, who had been educated at a training college in Halesowen. Her mother, who had spent her late teens and early twenties in Switzerland, supported her plans to study abroad in Italy and then Germany. While in Germany she was asked by friends to go to the theatre, but how could she explain she was not allowed? Then she fell in with a group of Theosophists (whom her parents believed to be cult-like because of their scepticism about religion). Soon Daisy was facing an identical crisis of faith to Helen. Her parents felt a quiet despair and prayed fervently for her salvation.

Richard knew better than to antagonise either of his daughters. In a letter to Daisy, he wrote: 'Times of trial and temptation and disappointment come to us all but there is sure refuge and strength in Him.' He continued, saying, 'Rest assured we shall not judge thee.' In response, Daisy promised not to visit the theatre while she was at home in Birmingham but reserved the right to do so while she was abroad.

Richard decided that what the family needed was another holiday together. The adverts for Thomas Cook's steamboat tours along the River Nile and the camping tours in Palestine looked immensely tempting to Richard. He had always been fascinated by the Egyptians; now he had the chance to see the pyramids in real life. This could then be followed by a pilgrimage to all the biblical places of the Holy Land, which would enhance his teaching of the Adult Class. Uppermost in Richard's mind, however, was the opportunity he saw to renew the bonds that tied the family together; it would, he hoped, be a way of bringing his errant daughters, Helen and Daisy, back into the fold.

For Beatrice this would mean yet more time away from school.

*

In early 1897 Beatrice, now thirteen, Edith, Helen and Daisy set off with their parents on a tour of Egypt and Palestine, travelling by boat to France and then by train to the Italian port of Brindisi.

It took five days to reach Port Said, whereupon the boat was 'invaded' by Arab traders offering to carry luggage and with armfuls of embroideries, carpets and jewellery to sell.

The family's first stop was at the peaceful and comfortable rooms of the Shepheard's Hotel in Cairo and from the front terrace Beatrice gazed out onto the crowded streets, noting, in her journal, the 'thronging mass of people and donkeys and mules'.

The heat was overwhelming the next day when they began the drive out of Cairo to see the Sphinx and the Pyramids. (On the way up the pyramid their guide was solicitous, repeatedly asking Beatrice, "I make you satisfied?" She nodded fervently, and he said, "Then you make me satisfied when we come down.")

Beatrice recalled crawling on her stomach through the hot and dusty narrow passages of the Great Pyramid to see the sarcophagus at the centre. To witness this first-hand beat school any day of the week. Another trip took them on camels to see the great head of the sphinx sticking out of the sand.

Next, they made a boat tour along the Nile on board the *Ramasses II*, a small steamer with capacity for about 50 travellers. Once back at Cairo they set sail again, this time to Palestine. They stopped first in Jaffa, where the famous orange groves greeted them. The taste of the sun-ripened oranges picked straight from the tree was delicious.

It took two days to get from Jaffa to Jerusalem, in open carriages. The first night they stopped in a German Hotel in Ramleh and then carried on through the Judean hills until the walls of the ancient city of Jerusalem came into sight. Beatrice recorded in her journal: 'I shall never forget what a moment of deep emotion this was for my father and mother, and indeed for us all.'

The next phase of the trip was a camping tour with their guide and interpreter, Ghalil Gandour, through all the biblical cities. First, they rode on horseback to Hebron and Jericho, and (of particular delight to Emma Jane) went bathing in the Dead Sea, where they floated seemingly miraculously, before later visiting the fresh waters fjords of the Jordan to wash the salt from their skin.

The first overnight stop was at Bethel. The tents and camping equipment were packed and sent on ahead so that the three sleeping tents, plus kitchen and dining tents could be erected ready for the family when they arrived at the site in the evening. Their cook prepared a hot meal for the weary travellers on his open brazier, and when the evening darkened, Richard – always the teacher – guided his daughters through the mysteries of the night sky.

As Richard had hoped, the tour succeeded in bringing the bible to life. Beatrice sat on the low wall of a deep well where Jesus, travelling from Jerusalem to Galilee, was said to have talked with the woman of Samaria.

The trip was not without its dangers however. The Cadbury party was advised to ride close together and to make as little noise as possible. Ghalil Gandour warned them the hill people of Jordan could be hostile to strangers, and on one occasion the family was pelted with stones, and their guide quickly led them to safety. There was no further trouble but it was a jolt to the party; a reminder that under a peaceful surface hostilities were ready to bubble up at any point.

They went to Damascus and took a day trip to see the wall and the ruins of the Temple of Baalbek. In Hermon they saw the giant stones on the way to the temple. As their trip drew to a close, Richard was keen to visit his first cousin, Caroline Cadbury, who was working at the Friends Mission Station in Brummana above Beirut. They caught the train from Damascus to Beirut and then travelled four hours in an open carriage through the orange groves and small villages to reach Brummana.

Thirteen-year-old Beatrice had been entranced by the holiday and looked forward to seeing one of her relatives on this last stop. They reached the mission station (which included a Girls

Training College and a hospital) and spent the final night with Caroline in the home of two missionaries, Dr and Mrs Manasseh. While the grown-ups discussed missionary work over their meal Beatrice gazed out at the twinkling lights of Beirut. And there, across the Mediterranean Sea, were the mountain-tops of Cyprus. That night in Brummana remained a cherished memory for ever. The imprint of it would be recalled fifteen years later when she returned with her husband.

*

But home and the factory beckoned, not to mention school for Beatrice.

The Bournville Works was thriving. In the late 1890s thought was given to a succession plan. (Richard had turned sixty and his brother George was approaching that landmark age.) It was decided that in the event of the death of either of the Cadbury brothers then the partnership would be turned into a limited company, with their sons Barrow and William, and Edward and George Junior becoming directors. While this blueprint for the future was being drawn up neither Richard or George, or any of their sons, had the slightest intuition that this plan would soon have to be implemented.

*

Beatrice tried to settle back down to school life. She had been absent for the entire spring term of 1897 and by the end of the summer term, Miss Japp wrote: 'Beatrice has done well this term but she appeared to work with less interest since her long absence'. That September Beatrice went into the Upper Fourth still smarting somewhat from Miss Japp's words but she successfully applied herself to her studies. By the middle of 1898 the improvement was noted.

The family had banked precious memories during their

travels through the Middle East, and by 1899 Richard was filled with wanderlust again. He wanted to repeat the experience of the Egyptian holiday of two years previously.

Helen and Daisy took breaks from their college studies, and Edith and her husband Arnold arranged to leave their one-year-old son, Dickie, with Arnold's parents so they could go too. With some difficulty, Emma Jane arranged for Beatrice to have yet another break from Edgbaston High School.

The party retraced their footsteps only this time with an extra member, son-in-law Arnold. As they journeyed once again up the Nile, Beatrice, Helen and their father, each began to suffer from a sore throat and a raging temperature. The locals called it Nile Throat. By the time they reached the Shepheard's Hotel in Cairo they were all feeling very poorly.

Richard was disappointed and quite distraught at the thought of being a burden or a wet blanket on this longed-for trip. Helen and Beatrice recovered quickly. Emma Jane reassured her husband over the following few days, as did Beatrice, that he should take time to get better. After a week, Richard, Helen and Beatrice were declared well enough to travel by the doctor. He said that the open air would probably do them good. That was all Richard needed to hear.

The party set off for Jersualem once more, stopping off at a hotel in Jaffa. By the time they reached Jerusalem Richard had relapsed; he was in agonising pain although he tried his best to hide it from his children. He could not swallow food and even sipping cool liquids failed to quench the fire that burned his throat. Although no-one knew it yet, Richard had in fact contracted diphtheria. And it would prove fatal.

In the early hours of the following morning, Beatrice and her sisters were woken by an urgent knocking on their bedroom door. It was their mother. "Come to your father's bedside," she said. A Dr Wheeler was attending to Richard; in his weakened state, he had suffered a heart attack and now lay unconscious in his bed.

The family's prayers could not revive him and later that day, 22nd March 1899, Richard Cadbury died. He was 63.

Grief felled the entire family. Dr. Wheeler arranged for the body to be taken to the hospital in Jerusalem and the days that followed had a strange and surreal quality. No-one could quite believe he was dead. Just days before, Richard had written a letter to his Adult Class.

> 'My dear friends, we are a long distance apart but feel sure that
> our thoughts and prayers bring us very near-together [sic]. We
> are about 450 miles from Cairo on this wonderful river which
> flows through a desert land.'

It was a cruel irony that this 'wonderful river' should be the source of the bacteria that would prove fatal to Richard Cadbury. His body could not be brought back for another month but it had been his wish to be buried in Lodge Hill Cemetery in Selly Oak, in Birmingham, at a private Quaker burial ground.

Richard had been the linchpin, the centre of the family home and Emma Jane found it impossible to comprehend that just three years previously they had been celebrating their silver wedding and looking forward to many more years of happiness. The heart had been torn out of the family.

By the time they reached Birmingham, Emma Jane was all but ready to collapse. There was an outpouring of grief in the press and from the Bournville workers. Letters arrived daily at Uffculme speaking of Richard's kindness and his inspiration and example to others, and this was some comfort to his widow.

As had been agreed previously, the partnership of Cadbury Brothers was dissolved and a brand new limited company was formed, with Richard's brother George and their sons – Barrow, William, Edward and George junior – also at the helm as directors. Shares in the new company were issued to family members. These shares were of two types: Preference shares, which gave a fixed dividend each year but carried no voting power, and Ordinary shares, which did carry voting power. The new constitution had a crucial stipulation: Ordinary shares could never be transferred to anybody outside the Cadbury family. This was to make sure that only family members could determine company policy and management.

Beatrice, who was now almost sixteen, had no understanding of the significance of these business discussions. She had no need to. Her shares, a mix of Preference and Ordinary shares, were put in trust for her until she reached the age of twenty-one.

Against a backdrop of grief both the family and the business were forced to move on to a new phase.

3
Dutiful Daughter,
1899-1907

RICHARD CADBURY'S DEATH left a gaping hole within the Cadbury family, forcing them to reassemble their shattered lives. At the factory, Richard's first-born son Barrow – now aged thirty-six – became company secretary. Barrow's younger brother William (still living in the family home at Uffculme at the age of thirty-two) took on added responsibilities.

But it was the women in Richard's life who felt his death most keenly – Emma Jane remained distraught that her husband had been snatched away in his prime. And Edith, Helen, Daisy and Beatrice were equally devastated. Life was full of sadness without their fun-loving and kindly father. He had been the instigator of the whirlwind holidays, the hot cross bun tree, the saviour and benefactor of the poor.

However, they knew they had to continue, and to deal with practical matters. Richard Cadbury's will was read on 17th April 1899, almost a month after his death. The gross value of his estate was calculated at just over £920,000, before tax duty. Emma Jane received a large financial settlement of four thousand pounds, plus nine hundred Preference Shares, which would be shared out amongst the children were she to die. But Uffculme, the family home, was left in trust to Barrow, with the option for him to purchase the estate should he choose. There was no question, however, that Emma Jane and her girls would be asked to find somewhere else to live. Richard's will stipulated that Emma Jane should stay at Uffculme until either her death or any subsequent marriage. In any case, Barrow and his wife Geraldine had no designs on Uffculme; they were perfectly content in their modest home, Rosemary Cottage, in Edgbaston.

The months that followed Richard's death were lonely. Helen immediately moved back home to look after her mother. (Emma Jane's own mother, now Granny Wilson, lived in a cottage not far away.) They all dreaded the first Christmas without him. It had been a family tradition to spend Christmas one year at Uffculme and the next at Uncle George's home, with Richard dressed up as a jolly Santa, distributing gifts to the children and grandchildren. Christmas 1899 was spent quietly at Uffculme.

*

The new century rolled in and life continued, albeit in a more muted way. Beatrice returned to Edgbaston High School. Emma Jane picked up the voluntary work she had started with the Mothers' Meeting in Highgate.

In 1901, Emma Jane, Helen, Daisy and Beatrice went on a pilgrimage to Jerusalem, staying at the same hotel where Richard had died two years previously. Some of the funds from his estate were used to build a wing at the nearby hospital to commemorate his name.

Another bittersweet moment in this sombre period was the engagement and subsequent marriage of William. He married Emmeline Wilson, Emma Jane's niece, at a ceremony held at Devonshire House, the Friends' Meeting House in London.

(William and Emmeline were not actually related by blood.) William had lived at home for most of Beatrice's life and although she was glad to see him happy, it was a wrench to lose him from the family dwelling.

It was decided that Beatrice should continue her education as a boarder at the Mount School in York, where Helen and her half-sister Jessie had attended. By now there was a new head at Edgbaston High School, a Miss Young, and she wrote in her final report: 'Highly satisfactory. We are exceedingly sorry to lose Beatrice.'

On 13th September, 1901, Emma Jane took Beatrice up to Yorkshire where she would stay for two years. It was the first time her Little B had lived away from home, and although Emma Jane tried to keep busy with her meetings and with the grandchildren, she knew she would miss Beatrice terribly. 'My heart was heavy when I left thee – but thy Father's God was with thee,' she wrote to her daughter afterwards, putting on a brave show. 'Thou had a very large place in all our hearts – and we miss thee – but are glad to have thee at school for thy own sake.'

The Mount School was formed in the 1820s by the York Quarterly Meeting and was overseen by Joseph Rowntree, the father of the man of the same name who founded Rowntree's of York, a competitor to Cadbury in the chocolate-making arena. The Mount was a strictly Quaker school, set up to address the paucity of girls' education. Non-Quaker girls were allowed admission from the 1850s onwards on condition that they used 'thee' and 'thou' (a linguistic anachronism maintained by the Society of Friends) and dressed plainly, 'so as not to set a worldly example to the rest'. Both Jessie and Helen as Old Girls reassured Beatrice that she would be fine.

There was a lot to take in as Beatrice was shown around the school: in the main hall two busts of the philosophers John Locke and Francis Bacon were an imposing sight. On the left stood the school library, the girls' playroom, as well as the dining room.

On the right was the kitchen, the housekeeper's room and the headmistress's study. The classrooms were upstairs, as were the bedrooms. All rooms had high windows to let in light and fresh air.

Although Beatrice was too young to appreciate it, schools like Edgbaston High and The Mount had been trailblazers in terms of girls' education during the nineteenth century. From the 1860s onwards small groups of women had their eyes set on entering university. Girton College, for example, had its origins during this time.

In the early days of The Mount the curriculum had been narrow and heavily academic, with a school inspector commending 'the small proportion of efforts devoted to accomplishments, and the large share to intellectual culture'. But in the latter part of the century pioneering teachers had introduced singing lessons and sport, by stealth at first. (Approval for a gymnasium was given only after women were accepted onto the school governing committee in the 1890s.) Nevertheless, the moral strictures were always present too. When a copy of *Jane Eyre* found its way into the school it was confiscated immediately. Shelley was also censored by the English teachers – thus ensuring his works became that year's essential holiday reading. By the time of Beatrice's arrival in 1901 the school was in the middle of a major building programme that would add much-needed space to the school.

Beatrice settled down quickly into the school's routines. She had developed a robust appetite since the early days of fussy eating and food was of good quality and plentiful at the Mount. Breakfast began at seven o'clock (eight in winter) with bread and potted meat. This was followed by 'elevenses' of bread and butter, then 'dinner' at two o'clock, and a light supper in the evening. Puddings were typically stodgy boarding school fare: tapioca, jam roly poly and buns, which gave some comfort against the bitterly cold and windy Yorkshire climate. A much-cherished Sunday afternoon treat was gingerbread or jam tarts.

Some of the more traditional rituals had been abolished shortly before Beatrice's arrival. The school crocodile – a nuisance to pedestrians on the streets of York – had always had potential for mischief-making as fake messages ('Go faster!' 'Go slower!') were passed down the line of girls. In addition, the much-hated system of ranking pupils according to their position in the class was replaced by three divisions: First, Second and Third. Beatrice was pleased to find herself placed in the top stream.

Girls had domestic duties, known as 'offices', which included tidying the classroom, dusting the piano ("Dust musically, I beg you!" one of the teachers implored) and running the school library. There were also a number of social societies on offer. Beatrice joined the Natural History Society, the Debating Society – where they discussed contentious issues such as women's rights – and the Poetry Learning Association. Beatrice's excellent memory made learning the required twenty-four lines of poetry a week almost effortless.

Beatrice's letters to her mother, written dutifully on a Sunday evening, document a cheerfully busy time where it was clear that extra-curricular activities proved more appealing than academic work. She was highly excited to have been allowed to join the wildly-popular Astronomical Society. Star-gazing through the telescope in the school observatory recalled nights with her father on their camping holiday in Palestine.

The hurly-burly of school life was probably the best thing for Beatrice; it helped to offset some of the grief of losing her father so suddenly. Her first letter home in September, addressed to 'My own motherie', would have reassured Emma Jane that her daughter was not *too* homesick. She recorded a blackberry-picking excursion to Skipworth Common, a nature table exhibition (for which she and her friends had won first and second prizes), and a thrilling hockey match played against the old scholars. 'I do love thee so,' she concluded, 'and I think of thee and dearest daddy all the time. Thy own little Beatrice.' By the following month she was complaining along with all the other girls about the cold weather and their fruitless efforts to keep warm.

But The Mount was not entirely closeted from the outside world. In 1901, the Second Boer War was raging in South Africa and Beatrice was inspired by tales of Emily Hobhouse, a British-born welfare campaigner, who sought to expose the appalling conditions faced by women and children interned in the British-run camps, especially at Bloemfontein, where disease and malnutrition were rife. Beatrice was profoundly moved by one particular lecture: 'We heard a good deal of Miss Hobhouse and the concentration camps: what an awful lot of deaths of children there have been in there, it is dreadful.' To Beatrice, Emily Hobhouse was a wonderful role model – passionate about the cause, keen to tackle injustice and the inhumane treatment of others, and beautiful to boot.

Beatrice was a reasonably academic scholar but she never quite made up the lost ground caused by the many interruptions in her schooling. Her school report from The Mount in autumn 1902, two and a half years after her father's death, was mixed. Music, particularly the violin, was excellent, and German (in which she came top of her class that year) was 'very good on the whole'. In French her pronunciation was 'good'. Algebra was only 'fair' and arithmetic 'marred by slight inaccuracies'. Even her English was 'weak'; her tutor commented that Beatrice 'could do much better work' if she applied herself. In the sciences she was 'sometimes good' but 'not always satisfactory'.

Her head of bedroom remarked: 'Has tried hard, yet bedroom sometimes noisy and untidy'. As this was her first time away from home without her nursemaid or the coterie of other servants this was perhaps unsurprising.

The consequence of this mediocre report was that Beatrice was moved into the Second division from the First – and therefore out of the matriculation class. This was a blow to her self-esteem and over the next two terms she renewed her efforts and tried to apply herself more assiduously to lessons. But it was difficult when there were so many joyful distractions to occupy her time: tennis and hockey matches, the various societies, excursions and rambles.

She enjoyed making her study more homely, by adding a new bookcase and some pictures on the wall and 'a photo of dearest Daddy on the table [she wrote to her mother] that makes it sweeter still'.

Now aged nineteen, Beatrice was passing from adolescence into adulthood and, almost inevitably, she began to take an interest in the 'worldly pleasures' that her father had once forbidden. As well as excursions to pick flowers – of which Richard would have heartily approved – there were parties to attend, with musical bands. Beatrice asked her mother to send her her 'white silk skirts' and another piece of white silk that she intended to use as a belt. She was also broke, she confessed. 'I seem to do nothing but ask thee for things in this letter mummie, but could thou let me have a little more money? I absolutely haven't got a farthing. I did have less this term, didn't I? And I had to pay all my subscriptions.'

Her final summer term at The Mount in 1903 was particularly special and included a trip to Stanford Bridge with all the 'Matries' (the pupils taking the matriculation exam) and the mistresses. Beatrice was delighted to be asked along even though she had not been entered for the exam herself.

It had been decided instead that she would try for Westfield College in London, where her sister Helen had studied. To gain admission there was the terrifying prospect of sitting the college's special entrance exam. It appears that Beatrice was coached heavily by Miss Sturge, the headmistress at The Mount, who had obtained some specimen papers for her pupil to go through. In June, just two days before the start of the three-day examination, Beatrice wrote to Emma Jane: 'I have been trying to look up for the dreadful entrance exam. Oh mummie dear how I *do* hope I shall get this.'

Afterwards, she was relieved that the papers were not quite as awful as she had feared, although she cursed her bad luck that, 'Of course they chose Russia for a map to put in places and rivers, etc. and I had hardly looked it up at all!'

On 1st July she wrote to her mother with the news: 'I have heard this morning about the Westfield exam. I have passed. Oh, I am so glad. I got very low marks for geometry, but still I am so glad I got through.' It seems some of her mistresses were surprised too. 'Miss Eddington asked me today if I was really going to Westfield and I felt so proud to be able to say I'd had a letter from the mistress.'

In September, 1903, Beatrice moved to London to begin her studies, once again treading the same academic path as her sister Helen. Westfield College was a women-only institution established in 1882 and affiliated to the University of London. Its site was based in the leafy borough of Hampstead and by the 1900s the area was already home to a number of intellectual and artistic groups.

If The Mount School had been a whirlwind of fun for Beatrice then Westfield College proved even more stimulating. She was immediately caught up in the hum of student life. 'I have so enjoyed all this week,' she wrote to her mother, who had been anxiously waiting for news, 'except I've been awfully frightened in some of the lectures! Chemistry seemed almost an impossibility so I have decided to try and do Latin instead.' Beatrice knew this would be a challenge as she had never studied Latin before. 'We had the first Logic lecture the other day – it will be very interesting I expect but we have an appalling essay to write every week and I'm hopelessly at sea over the one for this week so far!' Despite these protestations of being overworked, she had found time to play two hockey games in her first week even though the ground was 'just slush'.

The freedom of being in London – both personal and intellectual – was a delight for Beatrice. She relished going into the city with friends, dashing 'in and out of the omnibus', taking afternoon tea at Oxford Circus, and staying up talking with friends long into the night. ('I haven't been properly late to bed this week and I *will* try not to be.') She reassured her 'dear motherie' that she was taking her pills, most probably the homeopathic remedies and tonics Emma Jane was so fond of.

It was a pleasure to be able to decorate her own 'sweet' rooms: a study with an adjoining bedroom. A flower-stand was ordered from Liberty's and a carpenter came in to build a corner seat. 'I do love my little rooms so much – do *do* come soon.' She asked her mother to send some green ribbon to use as curtain tie-backs ('they do look utterly sweet and homelike') and also her tablecloths from the nursery. Her best friend was a girl named Nellie, somewhat prone to debilitating headaches, with whom Beatrice shared the parcels of chocolates her brother William sent from the Bournville Works.

But as well as all the fripperies and frivolities Beatrice was starting to attend lectures in politics. 'We went to a Poverty lecture at Devonshire House by Mr Masterman, author of *The Heart of the Empire.*'

C. F. G. Masterman had written his book in 1901 to express his deep concern for the problems of modern city life. At the same time her Uncle George had begun to implement his and her father's vision of a 'model village' at Bournville, which combined affordable social housing with pleasant green spaces, as an alternative to the overcrowded living conditions in the Birmingham slums.

Beatrice was becoming more socially aware, albeit in a modest way at this stage. In 1904 she and her friend Nellie attended a protest meeting against the Licensing Bill held in the Albert Hall. She gave a heady report to her mother: 'It was tremendously interesting and inspiring. Viscount Peel spoke for a long time and then John Morley, the Bishop of Kensington and Arthur Chamberlain … all the speakers were splendid.'

That year Beatrice studied a range of subjects, decided in negotiation with her mistress: Greek, Logic, Modern European History, Chemistry, English (Chaucer) and German. She also made plans to speak to the mistress about doing 'at least some of the Divinity next year – I should just love to. I shall beg her to let me.'

But she could never resist an invitation to be taken away from her studies. A trip to Kew, with another friend Mary, evoked powerful memories of her childhood home, Moseley Hall. (It was 'just glorious ... the woods were blue with bluebells.') They spent the entire day in the gardens and arrived back so late that she and Mary were forced to climb in through the lecture room window.

These were exciting times for women in higher education. Sexual inequality was being challenged and Beatrice was surrounded by intelligent, empowered women who would serve as role models. When one of her tutors, Miss Skeel, was awarded her D.Litt, (only the second woman ever to have received it), the momentous event was recorded in Beatrice's letter home:

> 'We all gathered in the passage and cheered and clapped and sang an ode which had been composed for her. After dinner we chaired her round the dining hall to "Hail the conquering hero comes". We got tea trays and shovels and pokers, the gong and the bell – anything that would do to make a noise with – everyone was just wild. Miss Strudwick beating a tea tray with a poker and Miss MacDougall banging on the gong! Then on Friday evening we had her over to tea at Dyndale and we all dressed up as different stages of women from prehistoric woman to D.Litt! Miss Strudwick let her hair down and arranged herself in a blanket as a prehistoric woman! Imagine it!'

Beatrice was overawed to be in the company of such powerful and inspirational women.

Other letters from 1904, the year in which Beatrice turned twenty, illustrated the gaiety of college life: thrilling tennis matches, birthday teas, banquets where she admired her friends' gowns with some wistfulness, always feeling a little insecure about how she looked compared to the others. Miss Skeel, she noted, was 'resplendent' in her scarlet gown. She begged her mother for more clothes – especially hats and sundresses – to be sent to London immediately.

As for Quaker worship, Beatrice had every intention of getting along to Young Friends' meetings, but there were too many other activities competing for her time.

*

Since Richard Cadbury's death five years previously it had fallen mainly to Helen to shoulder the burden of looking after Emma Jane.

But Helen was becoming disgruntled by the lack of stimulation in her life. After her father died she had dutifully rushed back to the family home, but although she loved her mother dearly she found life at Uffculme dull and empty after the hustle and bustle of the previous decade. She missed Richard's energy and zest, and even his stern moral influence, which she had once resented but had come to see more positively again.

Daisy was in Italy, Beatrice was in London. Now that all the elder brothers and sisters had married and left home Helen and her mother, bar the remaining servants, were like two coins rattling in an empty tin.

Beatrice always enjoyed getting letters from 'Len' (her pet name for Helen at this time.) In February 1904, Beatrice received some surprising news from her sister: Helen had met and fallen in with a man she had only just met. Charles Alexander was an American singer and evangelist, and one half of the Torrey-Alexander duo who were making a name for themselves all over the world with their Christian Evangelical Mission tours. Charles, who had been born in Tennessee in 1867, had a fine singing voice and this was matched by Dr. Torrey's superb preaching abilities. Together the duo toured Britain and went down a storm.

When Emma Jane heard the pair were coming to preach at Bingley Hall in Birmingham, she wrote and offered to help with organising refreshments for the event. With nothing else to do, Helen went along, too, and when Charles glimpsed her amongst a crowd of volunteers he was instantly attracted to her. For Helen, now twenty-seven and still single, the feeling was gloriously mutual. It was as if fate (or God) had answered the call to end her loneliness. When Charles proposed to Helen in the gardens at Uffculme she said "yes" immediately. Emma Jane was equally delighted. Charles was good-looking, charismatic and deeply devout. He was just the person to keep Helen on the straight and narrow.

In July 1904, Helen and Charles were married at the Friends Meeting House in Bull Street, Birmingham, where Beatrice once again was bridesmaid. As Quaker customs dictated, the ceremony was very simple without any formal order of service. The vast array of flowers was kept for the family home, Uffculme. Uncle George stood up and led the gathering in prayer, while the couple made their vows to each other. To Beatrice, the onlooker, it was reminiscent of the love that her parents had had – deeply romantic, based on common interests and purpose, as well as a shared physical attraction.

Helen now had work to do and was looking forward with immense excitement to playing the role of an evangelist's wife. This would involve travelling all around the world, but first the couple built a house within the grounds of the Uffculme estate. They called it *Tennessee* as a nod to Charles' place of birth and this would be their base to return to. Beatrice still had her college studies to complete but even so she felt a pang of regret knowing that 'Len' would no longer be living at Uffculme when she came back for the holidays.

Daisy returned from Italy to fulfil Helen's caring role at

Uffculme but then the following year she met and married Neville Bradley, the brother of Charles Alexander's best man. The once recalcitrant daughters were now firmly on the road to respectability.

Theoretically, Beatrice faced three choices once her time at Westfield College ended: stay at home and care for 'motherie', pursue a career, or marry. Whatever she might secretly have yearned for, she accepted her fate with equanimity.

It was her turn to be the dutiful daughter.

In 1905, Beatrice turned twenty-one and inherited the shares in the Bournville Works that her father had left in his legacy. She appears to have received 100 Ordinary Shares and 150 Preference Shares at this stage, but many more would come to her later. Her legal affairs were dealt with by a distant cousin, the solicitor, Walter Barrow.

In her final year at college, Beatrice was being courted by one of her tutors, Miss Maynard, to serve on the London Committee of the Friends Foreign Mission Association (FFMA) – a Society of Friends' initiative to bring the Quaker message to lands as far afield as China, India, Madagascar and Syria. She wrote to her mother unsure about whether or not to accept the invitation. In the end she declined – in any case, her mother needed her at home. Helen and Daisy had each taken their turn caring for Emma Jane and now it was Beatrice's time to say farewell to freedom. She was due to return to Uffculme immediately.

*

When Daisy had married, she and her husband Neville had been posted to Southern China as FFMA missionaries. Neville was a doctor and his job was to run a leper colony in Pakhoi, with Daisy for support. Daisy had recently had a baby and Emma Jane was aching to see her granddaughter.

At the end of 1906, Beatrice and Emma Jane made plans for a

round-the-world tour, the first stop being Pakhoi. They expected to be away for at least six months and, as the departure date drew near, mother and daughter felt the sparkle of enthusiasm for travel returning. Helen and Charles, who were on a worldwide preaching tour, agreed to meet up with them once they were in China. Beatrice's cousins, Eleanor and Isabel (Uncle George and Aunt Elizabeth's children) wanted to go to Pakhoi too.

They travelled on board a luxurious P&O cruise ship, stopping first at Ceylon. After a few days enjoying the comforts of a plush hotel it was onwards to Singapore and then north to Hong Kong.

From Hong Kong they travelled four hundred sea miles in a little steamer through the Straits of Hainan, round the Gulf of Tonkin to a remote village just outside the port of Pakhoi, in Guanxi province. Daisy and Neville lived in a large mission complex with their own generously-proportioned house with a garden tended by Daisy. A team of servants in the native dress of long blue coat and wide-legged trousers took care of all the other domestic duties, including the cooking. Beatrice's cousin, Eleanor, remarked in her journal on the contrast between 'the European houses … all white with verandahs and many windows, looking very clean and roomy compared with the native houses.'

Beatrice was enormously proud of her sister, Daisy, in the way she provided wifely support to Neville, and as a new mother. The baby, Marguerite, was a plump and bonny thing, with rosy cheeks and a charming temperament. No doubt Beatrice also felt a twinge of sibling envy.

Neville invited Beatrice to see inside the leper compound; somewhat nervously she agreed to explore what lay behind the forty-foot wall. Entry was through a gate and down a pathway arched by two magnolia trees with pink buds that blossomed in the spring. Groups of men, some with visible signs of the disease, tended neat vegetable plots where peas and beans entwined bamboo frames. Neville explained that the leper colony functioned as a small and self-sufficient community of its own.

Male and female leper patients were treated in separate wings of the compound. Neville was a pioneer in the use of disinfectant; the wards were scrupulously clean. Some patients functioned more or less normally, while others – particularly those in the latter stages of the disease – were disfigured by walnut-like protrusions or shiny red lesions. Some had lost their hands and feet; others had certain facial features missing.

Neville was determined that he and his hospital staff would treat the patients humanely and with respect, which was far from the case in a second leper colony further away in the village. There, one of the local leaders remarked that if he had had his way the lepers would all be thrown into the sea to drown. Neville had been given a nickname: 'I shang' ('Healing light'). Usually, he was referred to simply as 'Big Man' – not surprising to the blue-eyed Liverpudlian, who stood at six foot two.

Another innovation in the leper compound was a workshop. Here, the smell of sawdust and fresh pine was a welcome relief from the antiseptic stench of the medical ward. Beatrice was deeply impressed to see three leper sufferers at work: one carving the front of a cabinet door, another repairing a chair-seat and the third hunched over as he painted a wooden box. In a room next door the female patients worked on lace-making, producing table mats and handkerchiefs.

Neville explained that the goods they made were taken down to the port and sold to pay for medicine and food. This typically Quaker resourcefulness permeated the whole compound.

*

Emma Jane was intensely happy to be with her two daughters, Daisy and Beatrice, and thrilled when Helen arrived later with Charles. She reflected on how amusing it was to be surrounded by family so many thousands of miles away from Birmingham.

Now aged sixty-five, she was still in excellent health apart from the occasional pain in her hip.

All too soon it was time for Helen and her husband to leave for Canada. Shortly afterwards, in March 1907, Beatrice and Emma Jane set off for the next leg of their journey.

It was the family custom to sing their farewells, no doubt to the puzzlement of the local people. As they left the docks Beatrice and Emma Jane, both with fine singing voices, serenaded Daisy and Neville from the steamer:

We'll never say goodbye in heaven,

We'll never say goodbye.

For in that land of joy and song

We'll never say goodbye.

Daisy did not know it, but this occasion was even more poignant than she realised. It was the last time she would see her mother.

*

Emma Jane and Beatrice travelled to Japan and then sailed for Vancouver on the *SS Oceania*. They had arranged to meet Helen and her husband during the Canadian leg of Charles' Christian Mission tour. The cruise ship afforded them a delicious period of rest and luxury after the relatively simple living on the mission compound. During the daytime they lazed on deck, their heads filled with precious memories of their trip so far and with thoughts of the future. Emma Jane was pleased that Helen and Daisy, now Mrs Alexander and Mrs Bradley, had both sorted out their lives and made good marriages, particularly after their teenage flirtations with 'worldly pleasures'. Beatrice was more wistful; pleased of course for her sisters but wondering about her own prospects for finding a husband and having children. What if she were destined to remain her mother's companion for ever?

The following day, 21st May 1907, a storm was brewing by the time the ship reached the midway point between Yokohama and Canada. Rain lashed down all morning and drove the passengers off the decks and into their cabins below. The storm abated for a while and then became more ferocious during the afternoon, causing Beatrice to retire to her cabin all day with seasickness. At dinner, guests nervously watched plates and cutlery sliding across the tables. Emma Jane, it was later reported, announced she was going to write some letters. She walked down the chandelier-lit corridor, occasionally touching the walnut-panelled walls for support.

The writing saloon was situated at the bottom of a steep staircase. Emma Jane stood at the top, about to descend, when a sudden lurch of the ship threw her to the bottom.

She was carried to the medical room where the ship's doctor diagnosed severe concussion. His assistant, who was unaware of Emma Jane's Quaker beliefs, tried to force brandy into her mouth in the hope of restoring her. Beatrice was found and immediately rushed to the medical room to keep a night-time vigil over her mother. For the next few hours, Emma Jane drifted in and out of consciousness and as the new day broke it became clear she could no longer respond to Beatrice's urgent pleadings. She never regained consciousness.

A family friend, Sir Alexander Simpson, who was on board the ship saw to all the practical arrangements and remained close by to give moral support to Beatrice. She managed to write a letter to Barrow back home in Birmingham, and sought consolation in the fact that at last her mother was to be reunited with her father.

The week that passed before the ship could reach shore was wretched. Beatrice's grief hit her like a physical blow. She caught a chill – with suspected pneumonia – and the days passed in a feverish haze, Beatrice waking each morning to the fresh realisation that her mother was dead. She barely had the energy to leave her cabin.

Beatrice had the difficult task of breaking the news to the others: Helen and Charles in Canada, Daisy and Neville whom they had left so happily, and everyone else back home in Birmingham. There was no radio on board the ship and as soon as it reached Vancouver, Helen and Charles were cabled with the bad news. They were waiting to meet Beatrice when she arrived in Winnipeg a few days later.

Beatrice remained with the couple while they made the complicated arrangements to have Emma Jane's body brought home. The horrible parallel with their father's death abroad was all too apparent. Eventually Beatrice made plans to return to England and Helen cut short her Canadian tour with Charles to come back to Uffculme so the two sisters could sort out their mother's affairs.

In lonelier moments Beatrice wondered what else her future had in store. She was a young woman of twenty-three with no career aspirations and certainly no sign of a husband. And yet her expected role as her mother's companion had without warning been cut short. Would she ever make a good marriage like her sisters?

What else was a rich girl to do?

Part II
The Search for a Purpose

4
Man with the Violin, 1907-1914

BEATRICE HAD LOST her father and mother. Now, under the terms stipulated in Richard Cadbury's will, she was effectively rendered homeless. Barrow, being the eldest son, was the natural heir to Uffculme.

However, he, Geraldine and their children were happily settled in their Worcestershire home, Cropwood. (Their son, Paul, had contracted tuberculosis and the doctor had advised a move to the country for the benefit of Paul's health.) Privately, Barrow had always disliked the ostentatious Uffculme, so he was happy to take his father's lead in letting the mansion be used for the public good. An Adult School centre, he thought, would be a fitting memorial to his father's life.

During a short family meeting it was decided that Beatrice should move in with Helen and Charles to their home, Tennessee, within the grounds of Uffculme estate. The sisters had always been a close pair and Beatrice adored Charles, who liked to address her as 'my darling Betsy'. In many ways Charles reminded Beatrice of her father, and she grew to idealise her sister's marriage almost as much as she had her parents'.

But first there was the practical business of dealing with Uffculme and its contents. Beatrice and Helen returned to Birmingham and they began the sorry task of dismantling their childhood home. It would take four months in all. Charles was already committed to a tour of America during this period and was sorrowful at being separated from his wife. He wrote to Helen: 'My girl cannot go with me, and it is going to be a great wrench to pull apart'.

By the time Charles returned in September, Uffculme was closed off and the necessary alterations had been made to Tennessee to allow Beatrice to move in. Some, although not all, of the domestic staff from Uffculme were retained. Eliza Shrimpton, who had specialised in elaborate table settings at Uffculme, took over as parlourmaid and Emily Tipton (Tippie) became under-parlourmaid. Matilda (Orme) was in charge of laundry. They slotted in neatly with Helen's own staff, Fanny Wilcox, the cook, and Emma Blackshaw, the housemaid. In addition, Winifred Perks (Puckie) was on hand to help Helen and Beatrice with secretarial duties. Two of the gardeners also made the transition from Uffculme to Tennessee.

Beatrice's old nursemaid, the ever faithful Emma Denham, was asked to move in, rather to her surprise. But Helen and Charles were trying for a baby and, in the meantime, there were small nieces and nephews to welcome at Tennessee.

To occupy her time Beatrice picked up and continued Emma Jane's good work with the mothers at the Moseley Road Institute, as well as frequently attending meetings of the Gospel Temperance Mission. Her days buzzed with volunteering activity but finding an overall purpose was proving elusive, and there was little to distinguish one month from the next.

Charles and Helen announced their plans for a further tour of America in 1909, followed by another round-the-world trip in 1910, including stops in China, Korea and Japan. Helen felt awkward at the prospect of leaving Beatrice behind at Tennessee for such a long period and she invited her sister to go along with her and her husband. The impact of these trips on Beatrice was quite profound. She gained first-hand experience of the 'transformational' effects that preaching and mission work could have on people's lives. She also witnessed the devotion between husband and wife as Charles and Helen supported each other in their common purpose, in an echo of the relationship of her parents, Richard and Emma Jane.

By 1910 Beatrice was fast approaching the age at which Helen and Daisy had both settled down. But although she too was ripe for marriage, her prospects for romance were nowhere to be seen. She disliked the thought of becoming one of Miss Japp's Old Girls who let their brains wither while they waited for a suitor's proposal. Even more distasteful was the feeling that she was in the way as they toured the world, although her sister and her husband strongly denied it. Nevertheless, perhaps it was time for her to strike out on her own.

From Japan, Beatrice returned home alone. She spent two weeks on the Siberian Railway – a journey of almost 6000 miles – before changing trains at Moscow for Berlin. From Berlin she travelled to Ostend, where the flags were flying half-mast to mark the death of King Edward VII on 6th May 1910. Although desperately weary from her travels, by the time she reached Birmingham she had made up her mind: mission work would be her destiny.

*

Beatrice was already familiar with the work of the Friends Foreign Mission Association (FFMA), the Quaker organisation that trained missionaries in Great Britain and sent them out to selected countries to perform humanitarian work, such as building or managing schools and hospitals. This form of 'outreach' work had proved an effective way of spreading the Gospel message. The Quaker missionaries saw themselves as bringers of peace and goodwill; in their minds they were more tolerant of different religions than other Christian missionaries, many of whom had sanctioned forced conversions through brutal methods.

Daisy and Neville were in China working under the auspices of the FFMA, and Beatrice's Uncle Willie (her mother's youngest brother) and his wife Hannah had served in Madagascar, following Willie's decision to join the Society of Friends.

During her studies at Westfield College, Beatrice had resisted the calls to join; now she took the step of accepting an invitation to serve on the FFMA Candidates Committee, the sub-group responsible for appointing missionaries. The committee met regularly in London (at the Old Meeting House near Liverpool Street station) and its remit was to vet applicants thoroughly so as not to waste precious FFMA funds training the 'wrong' people.

Each FFMA territory (China, India, Madagascar and Syria) also had its own London-based committee. Having visited Syria with her father thirteen years previously, Beatrice readily agreed to serve on the Syria Committee too.

The FFMA had very precise requirements for its missionaries. They wanted 'healthy, happy, strenuous men and women, with personal knowledge of the forgiveness of sins, and full of faith.' As Beatrice began sifting through the applications, she realised just how well-qualified she was herself. She was exceptionally well-travelled; she had met and was comfortable with people of many races; she certainly had plenty of stamina.

And she knew her bible back to front.

*

Beatrice soon enjoyed her regular jaunts from Birmingham to London. As she boarded the train at New Street station, with her document case under her arm, she felt a sense of importance at last.

The task of the Candidates Committee meeting one day in 1910 was to select a Head Teacher to run the Boys' High School at Brummana in Syria. (Beatrice remembered clearly her visit to Brummana when she was thirteen.) The job was a challenging position, given the many religious divisions in that area, but would be an interesting role for the right candidate – someone with energy, enthusiasm and commitment.

There were several candidates to be interviewed. Along with the other members of the selection panel, Beatrice had scrutinised the application forms carefully beforehand. One of the shortlisted men was a Dutchman called Cornelis Boeke and, on paper, his academic credentials were good. He had been recommended to apply for the post by FFMA member and Quaker pacifist, Henry Hodgkin, whom he had met through the Student Christian Movement conference, of which Hodgkin was chair.

Mr Cornelis Boeke was called in. He was a tall young man, neatly turned out in a black suit, who strode purposefully towards his seat. His brown hair was combed away from his forehead and he wore an eager, intelligent expression on his face. Cornelis, who went by the nickname of 'Kees' (pronounced 'Case', he explained) was from Alkmaar, northern Holland, and the son of a Secondary School Head Teacher. He was a postgraduate student of engineering at Delft University, and his PhD was almost finished. Kees had visited England a number of times during his student days and had studied for a period at London University. Although his family were Mennonites, he had become increasingly interested in the work of the Society of Friends. He had realised he did not want to continue with engineering but was drawn more to the idea of mission work, particularly in the field of education. This post, he said, appealed to him because he had a profound interest in Arab people and the beauty of their language.

As Beatrice listened to this handsome blue-eyed man, with the disarming smile and impeccable spoken English, he began to have an intensely emotional effect on her. She was moved by his earnest sincerity and, although he did not know it yet, he had much in common with Beatrice: he too was 26, and also the youngest child of a large family. They shared the same love of music – he was an accomplished violin player as well as a pianist.

The interview was going well for Kees until it reached a stumbling block, which very nearly cost him the job. The application form had required the candidates to answer the question, 'Are you an abstainer from alcohol?'. (The Quaker creed required missionaries to be teetotal.) Kees answered honestly – no, he was not. Would he care to expand on his answer, one of the panel members asked.

Kees explained he was by no means a heavy drinker but had used alcohol occasionally. His instinct for truth-telling served him well on that occasion. The panel were won over by his frankness, as well as his enthusiasm and strong sense of purpose. The Head Teacher's post in Brummana was his.

To prepare for the job he would first have to spend a year in Birmingham doing his missionary training at the Woodbrooke centre on the leafy Bristol Road and its auxilliary college Kingsmead. Beatrice knew Woodbrooke very well – it was the former home of her Uncle George, and he had recently donated the building for use as a training college.

It looked as though she would have the opportunity to get to know Kees better.

*

At the beginning of 1911, Beatrice formed a study circle at Kingsmead to which Kees and his good friend and fellow trainee, Christofer Naish, were invited. Christofer was also going to be posted to Brummana. Beatrice told herself she had a 'special responsibility' towards both of them as she had been involved in their recruitment. But inside, her attraction to Kees was growing by the day. By June of that year, she had the first inkling that her feelings were not entirely one-sided.

During one of the bible study classes, Beatrice had introduced a textbook called 'Korea for Christ' that gave an account of the history of missionary work in that country, and which was prefaced by an account of her brother-in-law Charles's mission tour in 1909 (called, ambitiously, 'A Million Souls Campaign', because the target was to win a million Koreans to Christianity). Beatrice herself was mentioned in the book's introduction and she had secret hopes of impressing Kees.

After the class, Kees wrote a letter to his tutor, 'Miss Cadbury', to complain that the book 'Korea for Christ' was 'not considered a very suitable textbook for our study circle gathering'. In addition, he wrote '...there was a feeling of having too much foreign mission discussion. In any case I shall not accept your kind offer of lending some copies of the book'. Beatrice was flabbergasted. This was certainly not the response she had expected. Stung by his words, she read on.

Having criticised her teaching materials, he then asked her if she would pray for him, because he was due to speak at a forthcoming conference and he was a little daunted. He acknowledged he was making a 'very careless request' but, he continued, 'I do believe in asking the help by intercession on special occasions and of some special people with whom you feel spiritually united.' It dawned on Beatrice what Kees's true purpose for writing had been. His letter was the beginning of his courtship of her. Suddenly gleeful, she forgave him instantly for the gaucherie of his opening lines.

The June of 1911 proved to be a month full of dramatic events. Temperatures soared to record highs that year and against the backdrop of a sweltering heat the burgeoning romance between Beatrice and Kees was about to blossom. George V was due to be crowned on 22nd June and the whole country was in a frenzy of excitement. In the Tennessee household, a more personal but equally important event was imminent. Helen, who had finally become pregnant the previous year, was due to give birth and expected to go into labour at any moment. The nursery was already prepared and the faithful Emma Denham, now in her mid-fifties, was ready to resume her role as nursemaid to the Alexanders' first child.

On the eve of the coronation, Kees wrote again to Beatrice, revealing even more of his feelings. It was God, he said, who had 'sowed the seed of friendship and sympathy in human hearts' and been responsible for its growth. 'He has done it with you and me,' he stated firmly. On a more pragmatic note, he asked whether his mother, who was due to visit her son in Birmingham that weekend, might be allowed to call in at Tennessee and meet her, if only Beatrice could suggest a time. 'Please do not ring me up', he urged, 'but write, if you don't mind.' Kees was deeply attached to his mother, so if Beatrice doubted his seriousness then this request was proof of his intentions. A proposal of marriage would come soon.

But family matters at Tennessee were developing. On 29th June, after a long and arduous labour, Helen gave birth to a baby boy. Charles was joyous, proudly cradling his longed-for son, while his wife slept. Beatrice was equally moved by the sight of her dear little nephew. But there was a problem: the baby was small and weak, and he had breathing difficulties. Just hours after his entry into the world he died. Helen and Charles felt their dreams implode. They were utterly heartbroken and sought refuge in each other and in drawing on all their spiritual resources.

While this tragedy was being played out at home, Kees's letters became even more ardent. For Beatrice, her emotions were mixed, and it was a bittersweet period – grieving for her lost nephew one moment, yet thrilled the next by the fact that the man she was attracted to had fallen in love with her. 'Friendship comes unasked and cannot be rejected,' Kees maintained. 'No power can make it come ... but also no forces can possibly keep it out, when once its tyrant-will has decided to get in!' Kees was in the grip of a 'tyrant-will' and expected Beatrice to obey it too.

Beatrice had been unable to meet Kees's mother but by 4th July Kees had proposed to Beatrice. To his slight indignation, she asked him for more time to consider his proposal. What was holding her back when she was clearly ready for marriage and enticed by this passionate young man? Although apparently committed to Kees by this time, Beatrice's family situation was troubled. Helen, having just lost her baby son, needed Beatrice for support at home. The other troubling factor was that she had known Kees for a relatively short time. She needed time to think.

Kees, meanwhile, was rueing his own impetuousness. Lying awake in the early hours he composed a letter, writing: 'It was only a lack of trust in God's providence I think which made me wish for a sudden decision ...'

'From many little things I thought you had reached the same certainty and decision which I had had already for some time.' Implied in his words was an apology for not taking her doubts seriously enough. If he had seemed too pushy, it was only a result of his 'strong conviction' that God had brought them together. 'If even then you have the same doubt whether I shall be able to make you happy, do not decide rather than decide in what I believe to be the wrong way!' He asked her to bring the matter before God in prayer so that she would be convinced she ought to accept his 'desperately earnest' marriage proposal.

In looking to close all avenues that might lead to Beatrice saying no, Kees sought to reassure her that the 'abstinence question' (of alcohol) was as important to him as it was to her. To prove his seriousness over the issue, he recounted a tale of meeting a drunken man on the train from Coventry and appealing to the man to stop drinking.

The bombardment of letters continued in July, leaving Beatrice with little time for reflection. 'Please do not be angry with me for writing again,' Kees begged. With irrefutable logic, he argued that if Beatrice was worried about not knowing him well enough then 'the case [won't] become any better if we do not see one another at all.' He was desperately anxious to be allowed to see her again, and apologetic for having spoken too soon about his feelings, although this regret was tempered with a sense of pique. ('I apparently was wrong in doing so.')

Sensing that he might be winning, Kees made a bold request. Beatrice had told him that she would be going on holiday to Cornwall with Helen and Charles the following month. He invited himself. 'You would make me so happy for instance if you would allow me to go to the same seaside place where you said you would be going with your sister [Helen]. That would be a good way to really get to know one another, would it not? Do allow me this please! Oh, do not refuse this! Yours sincerely, Kees.'

When Beatrice finally said yes to his proposal, Kees was delighted and could not wait to broadcast the news. 'Before supper I told the joyful story to my dear mother, who had the [sic] tears in her eyes!' On 18th July, he declared: 'What a difference there is between a night now and before. Now it is only joy to be awake early in the morning.' He had won her hand in marriage and was suddenly light-hearted. Beatrice had corresponded with him on blue letter-headed notepaper and Kees could now joke: 'The nightmare created by the blue letter has disappeared and I won't let it come back. Please don't use the same paper when you write again; it will give me "the blues!"'

He was cock-a-hoop with the news – 'I suddenly break out laughing for pure, burning joy.' – and he wanted her to meet his mother in London, requesting that she left Helen for a day. ('Now it is your turn to be kind and do this for my sake.')

He had many romantic plans for their holiday, which Beatrice had finally agreed to. Although his 'poor fiddle' was in a sorry state, damp and with a string broken, he was going to play to her his favourite piece, Bach's *Ciaccona* – 'which is just about the finest piece there is for violin-solo. But I must practise first.'

Kees was utterly charming and she forgave the occasional

abruptness in his tone, excusing it by the fact that he was writing in his second language. She was enthralled by his sweetness when signing off his letters: 'I'll just end up in an ordinary way and you may read between the lines all the nicest things you can think of – even then you will only have a rather poor expression of what I feel. Yours sincerely, Kees.'

19th July became the official date of their engagement, after a courtship lasting a mere six weeks. Before the announcement could be made public, however, there was the matter of Kees being accepted into the Cadbury family.

The couple visited Uncle George at the Bournville Works and Kees was pleased that George was 'very, very kind' to them. It was an endorsement of their engagement when George said he felt sure that Richard Cadbury would have given his blessing on their decision to marry.

A further meeting was held at Tennessee for Kees to be introduced to Beatrice's siblings. Writing the next day, Kees thought that Edith and her husband Arnold were 'nice' and he had felt a real welcome from them. Helen and Charles were 'as hearty as anyone could be'. From others, however, Kees found there was 'more wonder, even a little spite than hearty welcome'.

'I know that it is only the result of their knowing how great my treasure is!' But inside Kees felt hurt. This made him peevish and rather tactless with his bride-to-be. 'The only thing … I cannot understand,' he ruminated, 'is how it is that such an angel has been waiting so many years until I should come! But I shan't worry about that, I can tell thee!'

One of the family members who advised caution about Kees was Barrow. In the absence of a father it was natural that Barrow should act in a paternalistic capacity for Beatrice. He asked the couple to wait before making their engagement public; he felt they were rushing into marriage. Beatrice understood her brother's feelings – they *had* rather taken the family by storm – but Kees was cross at this threat to his plans, noting in a letter written the day after the party: 'This conversation with Barrow did send a shadow over the bright sunshine of this whole God-given day … I must wait before I write to my family and my friends until he is satisfied and as the oldest brother has welcomed me into ɣ [sic] thy circle.' From this point onwards, Kees adopted the Quaker use of 'thou' and 'thee' instead of 'you' for second person singular pronoun usage. This above all demonstrated how far he was willing to bend in order to win Beatrice's hand. If Beatrice found his ardour a little overwhelming, she was still ready to leap into marriage. For her, their attraction was based on their common beliefs and ideals – it was truly a meeting of minds.

During the summer of 1911, they spent some weeks with Helen and Charles in Devon and Cornwall. Kees was still working on his dissertation in the mornings, and growing anxious about his submission deadline. But in the afternoons, he and Beatrice, chaperoned by the Alexanders, walked along the low walls between the cornfields, spotting blue butterflies among the ripening grain. Beatrice enjoyed showing Kees all the favourite haunts from her golden childhood, including Kynaston Cove, where they watched the gulls nesting. In the evenings he played Bach to her, as he had promised, but on a brand new violin that Beatrice had given to him as an engagement present. (It had cost one hundred pounds and she did not dare tell Barrow.) The sleeping arrangements were entirely respectable. Kees and his companion, a young draughtsman and illustrator of Kees's book, slept in a cottage in the village, while Beatrice, Helen and Charles stayed in a bungalow above the headland of The Lizard.

The couple had time to plan their new life together. Kees said, laughingly, to Helen and Charles: "Betty wanted to send me to Brummana, but instead I'm taking her with me!" In September, Kees would go to Syria first for a term to become acquainted with the work and to learn Arabic, returning to Birmingham in December so that he could marry Beatrice. (This was not Kees's original hope – he very much wanted to postpone his start date until the New Year so he and his new wife could venture to Syria together. He was worried about the travel costs and not being able to finish his thesis on time. The Syria Committee said no.) He was slightly sore about it and teased Beatrice that he did not think it necessary to go out first 'to prepare everything for thy Royal Highness (though of course I shall readily do so if you thinkest it right)'.

Kees was a man who liked his own way, and was aware of this tendency to self-centredness. A few weeks into their relationship he jokingly warned Beatrice, 'thou wilt have to change thy character, dearest' – he meant become a bit more assertive – otherwise, Kees believed, he would get 'worse and worse until I am a fearful brute, utterly selfish and inconsiderate for other people's interest!'

*

September arrived and Beatrice said farewell to Kees as he set off for Syria. The wedding had been set for 19th December – five months to the day of their engagement. The months leading up to the occasion were hectic and this made the pain of separation bearable for Beatrice. Charles was also touring again, this time without Helen, and the two sisters were brought even closer together. Daisy, her husband Neville and their children, arrived from China on leave and Beatrice prepared a house in Evesham for them to stay at. She welcomed all the distractions, although as soon as Kees's letters arrived she dropped whatever she was doing to read them avidly. In the days between his letters, she was sustained by recalling all the tender phrases he had written: 'Oh the feel of thy angel face – I know it so well already'; he wrote of wanting to 'whisper his love' into her ear, and of her 'true and shining star-eyes'.

19th December, 1911, dawned dark and rainy, but by midday, when the wedding party and the eight bridesmaids set off for the Friends Meeting House in Bull Street, the ominous clouds parted and the sun came out brilliantly. It was a good omen.

Kees made his vows solemnly: "Friends, in the fear of God and in the presence of the attendees I take Beatrice Cadbury as my wife, and promise, with God's help to be a loving and faithful husband for her, until it is God's will to us by death part." Beatrice made identical vows.

Kees's mother came to the wedding, as did around twenty of Kees's friends and other relatives from Holland. The couple had time only for the briefest of honeymoons at the Malvern home, Wynd's Point, before returning to spend Christmas Day at Tennessee.

All too soon it was time to embark for Syria to begin their married life in earnest. The trip was leisurely, beginning with a stop-off in Alkmaar, Holland, to visit Kees's mother. From there they went to Marseilles, via Paris, to catch the boat to Egypt, and from Cairo the couple visited the pyramids, allowing Beatrice to share her youthful escapades with her new husband. Finally, they caught the boat to Syria, stopping then in Beirut. Beatrice knew the journey to Brummana took four hours, as she had done it fifteen years before with her family. The open carriage train rocked through the mountains, passing the fragrant orange groves, olive hills and the whitewashed houses with their flat roofs. From the other side of the train, the Mediterranean sea stretched out. Beatrice was pleased though nervous to be returning, no longer as a child, but as the headmaster's wife – Mrs Boeke. It sounded very grown-up.

A committee of teachers and pupils from the girls' and boys' schools came to greet the newlyweds. Outside the school entrance, greenery arched over the gate, together with a painted card that read WELCOME. Beatrice was touched.

The couple's bulkier luggage, including a dining table and a full set of dining chairs, was transported entirely by camel. Even Kees's beloved new piano – a wedding present from dear Oma, his mother – was shipped to Syria and pulled up the steep hill to

Brummana. A friend remarked, drily, 'There can hardly have been more upsetting episodes in the life either of the piano, or of the camel!'

The boys' school had about seventy pupils, originating primarily from Syria, although some came from neighbouring countries. A few were wealthy – the sons of sheiks – while most were ordinary village boys from relatively humble households. One of Beatrice's duties was to go round at night and check the boys were in bed. Happily, so Kees would later report to the FFMA, the boys were, by and large, well-behaved. In his 1912 account, he wrote: 'There is much in the character of Syrian boys to make school life easy ... I almost wonder sometimes if they are really boys.' Kees himself had a strong mischievous streak. He went on, 'In fact, it almost makes me glad when I hear they have tied one of themselves to his bed during his sleep, or played some other boy's trick.' However, Kees played down certain incidents. Violence would occasionally break out between the school boys and the sudden appearance of knives and other weapons was alarming. Often it took the intervention of Kees or Beatrice to avoid bloodshed.

Mission work was arduous. The stated aim of the FFMA was to try to 'counteract many of the evils that characterise village life'; these 'evils' included general conflicts between the different religious groups, or more specific issues that had been identified by the FFMA, such as the high divorce rate within the Druze community – which had a devastating impact on women and children.

Beatrice and Kees's living quarters were modest: simply a large room, with a curtain to divide the sleeping area from the living area. All their meals, apart from afternoon tea, were taken with the boys in the dining room, seated at long tables. Beatrice admired the elegance with which the boys drank water, holding a jug high and letting the water 'flow into their mouths in a graceful curve'. Another pleasing aspect was the food. As she had always been revolted by meat, she found the simple, fragrant cuisine a delight: apricots, figs, orange and lemons, wholegrains and other unfussy foodstuffs.

Keen to fully embrace Syrian life, Beatrice and Kees embarked on a series of Arabic lessons to help them integrate fully into school and village life. The problem they faced was familiar to language learners. The locals were just as keen to practise their English as the couple were to speak Arabic, so progress was somewhat slow. Still, determined not to be the kind of missionaries who lapsed back into English, they took and passed their basic certificate in Arabic and resolved to carry on to the next level.

Beatrice watched with pride as Kees settled down to his teaching career. He had to prepare five hours of lessons a day, which did not seem overly burdensome to him, and it left plenty of time to devote to his new wife. In April, 1912, Beatrice discovered she was pregnant and wrote to tell Kees's mother:

> 'Dearest mother, I cannot wait any longer without writing to thee of the wonderful joy and hope that is ours … we believe and hope that God is going to grant us the wonderful gift of a life to care for.'

Kees thought it would be a splendid idea for Oma to travel to Brummana and support his wife during the birth. Beatrice was less keen. She was fond of her mother-in-law but she drew the line at her presence during these intimate stages. She tactfully explained to Kees that it would be better if her Aunt Hannah, Uncle Willie's wife, came to visit instead.

They soon developed a strong network of friends, including the head of the girls' school, Mrs Clarke, and the head of the hospital, Sister Ethel Stevens. Chris Naish, who had studied with Kees at Kingsmead, was also in Brummana, and they had Syrian friends too, including Nageeb Karem and the Manassehs. Beatrice enjoyed the evenings best, as they sat gazing out at the terraced hills planted with vine and mulberry trees, which fed the silkworms. (Spinning and weaving silk was the chief industry, Beatrice had discovered). Sitting with her hands on her swollen tummy, she felt deeply contented and grateful for the way her life had turned out.

*

During the summer holidays of 1912, while Beatrice was in her second trimester, she and Kees holidayed in Baalbek. Here, the heat was so oppressive that Beatrice struggled to cope. Their hotel room had a tiled floor and Kees repeatedly tipped buckets of water over it to try and reduce the temperature for Beatrice, only to find that the water evaporated within minutes, effectively turning the room into an unpleasant sauna. She felt unwell and they returned to Brummana ahead of schedule, whereafter she seemed to recover.

On 11th November their first child was born; a little girl, whom they named Helen, after Beatrice's beloved sister. Shortly after the birth, which had been difficult but just about bearable, the couple had a devotional meeting to give thanks for the baby's safe arrival. The message did the rounds of Brummana ('Only a girl, never mind!') but this could not taint the couple's delight.

A few days later, Beatrice was struck down by illness. The doctors were slow to recognise the cause, assuming it to be a reaction to the strenuous birth. As Beatrice lay feverish and delirious in her bed, a special doctor from a medical college in Beirut was called in. He spotted immediately that it was typhoid. The source of the disease probably originated in their trip to Baalbek, where it had lain dormant in Beatrice's system for months.

It was an anxious and terrifying few weeks. Kees did his best to carry on with his teaching and headship duties, while baby Helen was nursed by Mrs Clarke from the Girls' School. On hearing of this dreadful news, Barrow immediately sent over a nurse to care for Beatrice. William, her second eldest brother, and her doctor brother-in-law Neville (Daisy's husband) came out to Syria, bringing another nurse with them.

It was a desperate time, not just for Beatrice's family in England, but for the whole Brummana community, who had embraced Beatrice warmly. The FFMA report of 1913 spoke of the 'heavy cloud' they were under, because of 'Mrs Boeke's severe illness'.

Thanks to the swift medical intervention Beatrice received, she gradually began to recover. But she had missed all her bonding time with her baby daughter. They had spent three months apart and their eventual reunion was far from the joyous occasion that Beatrice had anticipated. She later wrote, 'What was my acute and bitter sorrow when, since to her I was a perfect stranger, she began to cry when she was put in my arms. Her tears and mine flowed together.' The illness left Beatrice looking skin and bone and the following March, when the Boekes went to Holland and England to help her recuperate, all the relatives were shocked by the hollow-eyed fragility of her appearance.

By the time they returned to Brummana, Kees's position as head of the Boys' School had been filled without his knowledge, and he was moved further inland to the town of Ras el Metn. His job involved travelling by donkey around the different villages, in an inspector's role, monitoring the day schools. It felt like a step backwards for Kees.

Here, it was more difficult to integrate. Although Beatrice remarked on the unfailing courtesy of the local people – who belonged mainly to the Druze community – they were difficult to read behind their gracious facades. There were countless sessions with the village women, where she was forced (out of politeness) to drink endless cups of coffee and eat platefuls of biscuits, only to find her relationship with them had not progressed one jot. In Beatrice's presence, the women usually removed their veils, but Kees took a mischievous pleasure in suddenly appearing around the corner and watching them hastily cover their faces again.

But at least the couple's commitment to learning Arabic was paying off. Kees was fluent enough for him to give addresses in Arabic during meetings and even baby Helen was beginning to babble happily in English and Arabic, to the proud delight of her parents.

After a year, they decided they wanted to go back to Brummana. Kees did not find his current job stimulating or pioneering enough and they began making plans to return. But in early August, 1914, the couple received unexpected and alarming news. Germany had invaded Belgium, and England had declared war on the aggressors.

They had been so engaged in their mission work in Syria they had not been kept abreast of the political situation in Europe. To Beatrice, it seemed incredible that these famous cities – first Belgium and then Paris – had been invaded. As the weeks went by, it seemed likely that nearby Turkey would join in on the side of Germany. As a result, all British citizens were strongly advised to leave Syria immediately.

This caused a dilemma for the couple. By virtue of marriage to Kees, Beatrice had been registered as a Dutch citizen when she arrived in Syria. Holland was neutral so they had protection – in theory. But the couple were told by the British Consulate in Syria to leave anyway. "You work for an English missionary society," he said, "and it will be better for your Arab friends not to have personal relationships with English people." Very reluctantly, Beatrice agreed it would be wrong to compromise the safety of their Syrian friends, however much she wanted to stay. Another deciding factor was that Beatrice was now expecting their second child, due in November. They would go back to England, reassured by claims that the war would be over in a few months. They said their farewells, and promised to return soon, this time with their two children.

Travelling home by train through Europe was considered too

dangerous, so the Boekes had to make the journey to England all the way by boat. The Mediterranean Sea was occupied by German cruisers, so they had to travel at night without lights, through the Mediterranean, round Gibraltar and via the Bay of Biscay, before docking safely at Southampton. Barrow and Helen were waiting at the port for them, anxious to see for themselves the safe return of their sister and her daughter and husband.

However, this was wartime and suddenly everybody was under suspicion. Because their papers were Dutch, the three of them were not allowed to disembark with all the other passengers. Instead, they were ordered to stay on the boat until it reached London, where they would have to get their official papers. It was a foretaste of trials to come with the British authorities.

Eventually, the travel-weary trio arrived in Birmingham and soon settled back at Tennessee. The servants made a huge fuss over little Helen, and clucked over Beatrice, the expectant mother. Beatrice and Kees still hoped to be back in Brummana before Christmas, but as time passed their hopes began to dissipate. The next four years would be their most testing time yet.

5

'The Germans are our brothers',
1914-1918

BEATRICE HAD BECOME used to the relative simplicity of her lifestyle in Brummana and Ras el Metn. Now, back at Tennessee with Helen and Charles, her living conditions seemed lavish in comparison; but after a week or two she began to enjoy the attentions of the servants as she prepared for the birth of her second child (hopefully, a boy this time).

Beatrice's days passed happily that September. Mornings began with breakfast in bed for the expectant mother, followed by a period of letter writing or, occasionally, a shopping trip to Liberty's to buy clothes for the baby. In the afternoons, her time was taken up welcoming callers, friends and family, who would take tea in the nursery with her and little Helen. The toddler was a chatty, sociable child who attracted friends wherever she went. With her mother's fondness for animals, she loved nothing better than being taken out to see the animals on the Uffculme estate, now serving as a convalescent home.

The war did not touch the Boeke family at first. In the autumn months of 1914, Beatrice was more concerned about arrangements for the new baby, particularly finding a suitable nanny. One of the Tennessee staff, Mrs Harrison, had been looking after little Helen, and it had been a satisfactory arrangement. But Mrs Harrison was now pressing for a higher wage and Beatrice was inclined to say no. Rather than begrudging the salary increase, it is more likely Beatrice refused because she had plans to employ her own nursemaid, Emma Denham, this time to care for both Helen and the new baby when it arrived. Now approaching sixty, Emma Denham had been caring for her sick mother, but that October – a month before the baby was due – she was persuaded by Beatrice to return to Tennessee. Beatrice felt there was a pleasing sense of continuity that her own children would receive the same loving care from her dearest childhood nanny.

Emma Denham's first night was a disaster. Two-year-old Helen, perhaps predictably, was deeply upset to have a strange old lady in place of her beloved Mrs Harrison. She wept all through her bath-time.

*

On 21st November, 1914, shortly after Helen's second birthday, the new baby was born at the Tennessee house. It was another girl – although this time there were no Syrian friends to declare: "A girl? Never mind". Beatrice named her daughter Emma, after her own mother and grandmother. (The baby's other namesake, Emma Denham, was secretly pleased.) The only matter to cloud Beatrice's joy was concern for her sister, Helen, and her husband, Charles. She knew the birth of Emma in their home would have been a bittersweet reminder of the loss of their baby son, especially so as Helen and Charles had, by now, realised they would never be blessed with children of their own. But Helen reassured her sister and proved to be a loving aunt.

Meanwhile, Charles still had his own missionary work to do and his next assignment called him back to America. Naturally, he wanted his wife to go with him, and on 16th December, 1914, the couple sailed for New York, on board the *Lusitania*, leaving Beatrice, Kees, and their two daughters at Tennessee. The Alexanders would be back by the following April but in the meantime the Boeke family had the whole house to themselves.

*

The early prediction that the war would be 'over by Christmas' had proved spectacularly wrong. From the very beginning of the conflict, a groundswell of opinion had begun to mobilise in opposition to the war. Quakers did not fight. This was the traditional position enshrined in the Peace Testimony of the Society of Friends. The Quaker principle, based on the teachings of Jesus, renounced violence of any kind and challenged the rights of governments to say 'You shall bear arms'. The outbreak of war in 1914 brought this creed into sharp focus.

As far back as 1911, prominent British Quakers had discussed what their response should be if war broke out. By 1914, members of the Society of Friends articulated a range of positions. Some felt they *would* sign up to fight, for the greater good of mankind. Others were called instead to relief work for organisations like the Red Cross, or the Quaker groups: the Friends' Ambulance Unit and the Friends' War Victims Relief Committee. A third group, however, could not support the war on any grounds, under any circumstances. Their totally pacifist stance earned them the nickname of the Absolutists. The war ensured that sooner or later every Quaker would be forced to consider their stance – Beatrice and Kees included.

*

At the beginning of the war, a group of Christians from different denominations quickly banded together to form a group called the Fellowship of Reconciliation (FOR). The organisation's aim

91

was simple: to oppose war on Christian grounds. Its activities included press campaigns, pamphleteering and, later, preaching in the streets to broadcast the message of peace.

Many prominent Quakers were instrumental in setting up the FOR. Henry Hodgkin (who had supported Kees's application to the Syria Committee) was a key player, along with the German Lutheran, Friedrich Siegmund-Schultze. The two men had attended a peace conference in Konstanz, Germany, in August 1914, just before the outbreak of war and, as they parted company at Cologne train station, Hodgkin and Siegmund-Schultze shook hands and made a pact: "We are one in Christ and can never be at war." Beatrice and Kees, still in touch with Henry Hodgkin, joined the FOR in 1915 and a Birmingham branch began, where Kees was appointed Secretary.

At the start of the war the country seemed gripped by a patriotic fervour, but as Britain had only a small professional army the government relied on moral pressure to encourage young men to sign up. *Come into the ranks and fight for your King and country – Don't stay in the crowd and stare* ran the slogan of a typical propaganda poster. Another poster said: *Every fit Briton should join our brave men at the Front. ENLIST NOW.* For many young men, the promise of glory was seductive; the thrill of wearing a soldier's uniform brought approval, validation and a strong sense of pride. The government's appeal for young men to do their duty worked successfully – to begin with. But what would happen when the armed forces ran out of willing men?

The FOR foresaw the introduction of Compulsory Military Service (which was not officially declared for single men until January 1916) and intended to thwart it from the outset. The organisation sought to give a voice to the Conscientious Objector, the CO for short, who may have been a person of faith but, equally, could be any young man who did not wish to fight, but who had not yet learned how to articulate his objection.

The FOR was in contact with another pressure group, the

No-Conscription Fellowship, also formed at the start of the war, and supported by key figures like the philosopher, Bertrand Russell. At the Birmingham FOR branch meeting, Beatrice and Kees heard reports of a London meeting of the No-Conscription Fellowship, attended by over 2000 men, each of whom were undecided about whether or not they should enlist. The men were looking to the leaders, Fenner Brockway and Clifford Allen, for guidance. But outside, a braying mob, filled with righteous indignation towards the 'cowards' inside, shouted and brawled and banged on the windows. The meeting had to abandon any applause and the audience were guided to show their reactions by waving their handkerchiefs in silence. Many men came away from the meeting more convinced than ever that war was morally wrong. Yet the pacifist stance took great courage. Objecting to the war was a lonely business and COs faced vilification from almost every direction.

*

The Cadbury family was challenged as much as any other family by the outbreak of war. Feelings ran high on both the pro- and anti-war sides and the war would put each of them into different camps. Like Beatrice and Kees, Barrow was sympathetic to the FOR and the early accounts of the organisation show that he made a generous donation of five hundred pounds to support its work. Uncle George, too, was a life-long pacifist; but two of his younger sons (who were not working at Bournville) had different views. His youngest, Egbert ('Bertie'), enlisted in the navy, where he worked as a mine-sweeper in the North Sea. It was hazardous work, although Bertie endeavoured to play down the dangers so his parents would not fret. ("Don't tell Mother or Father", he instructed his brother, Lawrence, after a particularly risky operation.) Later in the war, Bertie would join the Royal Naval Air Service to counter-attack the German zeppelins.

Meanwhile, Beatrice's other cousin, Norman – Bertie's younger brother – was an engineer by trade, like Kees, and he went to work at a factory manufacturing military equipment, including bombs. To Beatrice and Kees, who were beginning to maintain an Absolutist position on the war, this was abhorrent. Her third cousin, Lawrence (Uncle George's eldest son) adopted a compromise position. Like many Quakers that were opposed to the war, he still wanted to do something and he was recruited to the Friends' Ambulance Service, treating wounded soldiers at Dunkirk and then Ypres, witnessing first-hand the horrors of war.

The Cadbury factory remained open throughout the war, albeit with a much-depleted workforce. They aided the war effort by sending food parcels out to the armed forces and then, under government orders, switched some of their chocolate production to milk, butter and cheese, as well as some biscuits and dried vegetable foodstuffs.

*

By the middle of 1915, Beatrice and Kees wanted to take a more active role in peace campaigning. Kees needed to do something. In England he was enervated by boredom. Being without a purpose did not suit his forcefully energetic personality. (He also enroled on a year-long teacher training course at the University of Birmingham, to study for a Secondary Teachers' Diploma. His teaching practice included several months at Walsall High School for Boys.)

After he became secretary of the Birmingham branch of the Fellowship of Reconciliation, Kees met members of other FOR groups at a national level. During one of these meetings, he was asked by the committee if he would be willing to travel to Germany and make contact with German anti-war campaigners.

Kees was ideally placed to travel across Europe. Because he

was a Dutch national, and Holland was neutral in the war, he was confident he could enter Germany without being questioned. He had the added advantage of being a German speaker. Even so, it would be a dangerous enterprise. He discussed it with Beatrice and she told him he should go, but members of the extended Cadbury family were worried. Of Beatrice's siblings, only Edith and her husband Arnold seemed to understand and be sympathetic to Kees's actions; the rest of the family, especially Barrow and William, advised caution. Regardless of the risk, Kees went anyway.

That July, Beatrice stood at Birmingham New Street station with toddler Helen wriggling in her arms, bidding goodbye to her husband. (Baby Emma was left in the care of Emma Denham.) The threesome stood amongst the throng of khaki-clad soldiers, who were saying similarly poignant farewells to their relatives. Helen asked "Where's daddy going?" as she watched Kees retreat. As soon as the train pulled out of the station, he put pen to paper.

'My dearest one,' [he wrote to Beatrice] 'I have again that strange empty feeling which always comes over me when I have left thee ... like waiting for a meal which does not come.' Beatrice returned to Tennessee and bore his absence stoically. If anything, she had encouraged him to go, knowing that he had a purpose to fulfil. Although she was worried, deep down there was a trust and a confidence, borne of her strong religious belief, that Kees would be alright. She replied to his letter, saying: 'My darling, I long to hold thee in my arms and yet I am glad and so proud of thy going.' Later, she reiterated her feelings. 'I rejoice in thee going.' Relatives thought she was being naïve to the risks, but in her mind her husband was making an important contribution to the peace effort and for that she was proud of him.

While Kees was away, life carried on as usual at Tennessee. For Beatrice this meant attending FOR meetings, taking the children away on short trips, having singing lessons, and – her latest hobby – trying to master photography with her expensive new camera. Two weeks after Kees had left, she made a thrilling discovery – she was pregnant again. By this stage of the war, the couple knew that all letters to and from abroad would be subject to the scrutiny of the censor. When Beatrice wrote to her husband to tell him the joyful baby news, she coded it carefully: 'I am *very* well,' she wrote.

In August, Beatrice took the children on holiday to a cottage in Nevin, North Wales. When they returned to the cottage, after a day spent pottering on the beach, Beatrice was alarmed to find a policeman on the doorstep wishing to interview her about her husband's activities abroad. The policeman explained that Mr Boeke's letters from Holland (where Kees had been staying with his mother before heading for Germany) had been opened by the censor and the authorities were suspicious. Could she, his wife, confirm the exact purpose of his trip?

Beatrice spoke truthfully, and with a hint of pride. "My husband is carrying out peace work in Europe." Somewhat non-plussed by her answer, the policeman nodded and went away. Nothing further happened during the holiday, and Kees was set to return the following month, so Beatrice dismissed the episode from her mind.

When Kees arrived home in September, his spirits were buoyant. The mission had been a real success, he told his wife, while Helen climbed all over daddy and dragged him to the nursery for tea and cake. Later that evening, as the couple chatted, Beatrice realised how dangerous the trip had in fact been. When Kees had gone to the German Consulate in Holland to arrange his travel papers, the official noticed from Kees's passport that he had travelled from England. This put him at risk of immediate arrest. The official, perhaps won over by Kees's frank manner, suggested he get himself a new passport, issued in Holland. He did so and was still able to keep his British-issued passport. This trickery enabled Kees to move freely throughout Germany, without attracting suspicion.

Beatrice could tell the trip had made a huge impression on Kees. He met prominent pacifists such as Elizabeth Rotten, a Quaker from Switzerland, who had undertaken the task of helping prisoners in Germany. Kees had visited church ministers, and made contact with political figures such as the socialist, Eduard Bernstein, who was vocal in his opposition to the war. In Berlin, he was awed to have spoken to Friedrich Siegmund-Schultze, the friend of Henry Hodgkin. All over Germany there were pockets of opposition to the war, voices willing to speak out, just as there was in Britain. Kees's face was ablaze as he related all this to his wife. Then he told her the problem he had almost had trying to get back into Britain.

He had taken the precaution of using his British-issued passport again. Even so, he was stopped at customs and had to face questions.

"Have you travelled further than Holland?" the passport official asked.

"Yes," Kees replied, confessing that he had been all over Germany and had been able to do so because he had both a British passport and a Dutch passport. He was lucky. His tactic of telling the truth in an apparently guileless manner, along with his winning smile, was successful this time. Kees was allowed through customs to return to Birmingham and be reunited with his family.

*

Meanwhile, the Conscientious Objection movements were gathering momentum but, as they did, so the British government began to crack down hard. Many anti-war protesters were imprisoned and portrayed as cowardly enemies. The battle of ideology raged just as fiercely as the physical battles on the Western Front. For every propaganda poster that glorified the war, the pacifist movements sought to counter it in equally robust and stirring terms.

The moral argument against the war was clear to thinkers like the Quaker pacifist, J.W. Graham, who later articulated his belief that war represented a reversal 'of every moral law', and 'of every habitual mental attitude of civilised man'. Instead of labouring to preserve life, to help the weak, to avoid lies, war had the opposite effect. Any good man would want to revolt against what Graham called 'this hideous organisation of wickedness'. The nation was deceived about the true facts of war; it was veiled in propaganda and people were 'stimulated daily' into fear and suspicion of the Germans by the newspapers. Furthermore, ran the pacifist argument, the war was caused not by ordinary people, but by leaders motivated by their own political ambition, their hatreds, and their fear of class and revolution.

Now, along with the Christian objection to war, Beatrice and Kees became exposed to new and hitherto unexplored ideas about class warfare. Socialist and class-based articulations against the war joined forces with the religious and moral arguments.

In October, 1915, Kees began work at a private school, The Woodruffs, teaching pupils aged nine to fourteen. Beatrice was pleased to see her husband working again. Christmas passed by with little cause for celebration while the war dragged on. There was the new baby to look forward to, however.

On 18th January, 1916, Beatrice's third child was born; another girl, named Paulina (Paula), after Kees' sister-in-law. Her birth coincided with the first zeppelin raids in the Midlands. From their window at Tennessee, the couple witnessed the falling bombs, and heard the ear-splitting explosions, followed by raging fires in the skyline as buildings caught fire. Tennessee had a cellar and the Boekes and their staff were braced to go down there but in the event the bombs came no closer than Walsall. They waited anxiously. Was the war ever going to end? Then, in the same month, the government announced conscription would be formally introduced under a new Military Services Act. It was a severe, although not unexpected, blow to the pacifist movements. The peace groups mobilised and pressed for fair and proper tribunals where the COs could make their case for refusing to serve.

By now, Beatrice and Kees were no longer content simply to discuss the issue of war in meetings. Kees began making public speeches at weekends. An early draft of one of these speeches, prepared for a Birmingham FOR rally, began with the words, 'To friends the world over, and to all those who seek the way of life, we have missed the way. Is it not time to set about seeking the god (of humanity) together?'

While Beatrice was busy with Helen, Emma and the new baby, Kees continued his post at the Woodruffs on weekdays. At first, he was an asset to the school, especially with teachers now being in short supply. He taught a wide range of subjects and encouraged out-of-school activities, including events and a hobbies exhibition held on the lawns of Tennessee, (rather echoing the days of Beatrice's father, Richard).

But then the trouble began. As part of Kees's teaching responsibilities, he was asked to take the lessons in scripture.

"The Germans are our brothers," he told the class. He pointed the pupils towards the bible passage from The Gospel of Matthew which recorded Jesus's Sermon on the Mount. "Love your enemies," Kees said, "and do good to them that hate you." Confused at how to interpret this message, some of the boys went home and told their parents. Before long, a deputation of parents arrived at the school to register their objections. They were not paying the school to instil their children with German propaganda! Kees agreed to resign, although Beatrice was fiercely loyal to him, and was immensely cross at the unfair way he had been treated.

At least now, she argued, they were free to throw themselves into working for the FOR with greater commitment.

It was in this same year, 1916, that Beatrice began to question her own rather lavish lifestyle. Living at Tennessee with its coterie of servants and fine furniture was all very nice, but it seemed wrong when balanced against the horrific stories that were coming back from the war zones and from civilian populations in Europe. Suddenly, Beatrice found she had lost her taste for the pampered surroundings offered by living in her sister's home. She was also aware that, in demonstrating more forcefully against the war as she now wanted to do, she might 'compromise' her sister and the reputation of the Cadbury name if she stayed at Tennessee. Furthermore, Beatrice was yearning for the friends they had been forced to leave behind in Syria; she had heard troubling reports that American missionaries had been forbidden to carry out relief work there. Writing to her husband, when she took a short trip to Wales with the children, she said:

> 'It seems almost wicked [for us] to be out of it all, and that
> we should have everything and more than we need, while our
> friends are literally starving.'

From America, Charles had sent Beatrice a copy of the evangelical Christian magazine, The King's Business. She had read it and was moved, she told Kees, by the 'very brave, outspoken editorial' on the Christian position on war. 'It quotes from Bertrand Russell (!) showing how futile and untrue is the argument of the "enobling influence of war".

*

In the summer of 1916, while Helen and Charles were still in America and unable to return, Beatrice and Kees decided to move out of Tennessee into a modest (by their standards) house at 52 Anderton Park Road in Moseley, Birmingham. On hearing of this surprising decision, Charles wrote to Beatrice ('My darling Betsy') from America to say she must take whatever she needed from the Tennessee house, including any of the servants. But Beatrice gracefully declined – she was ready to be independent.

By this time, Beatrice had made friends with Eveline Fletcher, who was planning to move with them into the new house and be on hand to help with the children. Ernest and Eveline Fletcher were a Church of England couple struggling with their own convictions about entering the war. In May, 1916, when conscription was extended to include married men, Ernest had refused to obey the conscription order and was imprisoned in Portland Prison in Weymouth. A photographer by trade, he would later become a key figure in the anti-war movement. Ernest was relieved to hear his wife Eveline had moved in with the Boeke family while he was serving his jail sentence.

During this time Beatrice also offered her help to the Friends' War Victims' Committee – an organisation set up to support the wives and children of 'enemy aliens', that is, men of German, Austrian and Hungarian origin living in England at the time of the war, who were interned in camps. She and a team of other volunteers worked to give practical support (food, clothes and other handouts) as well as moral support, advice and sympathy.

*

The COs became a severe irritant to the British authorities. It is estimated there were around 16,000 COs when conscription was introduced in 1916. Often they were just as patriotic and loyal to their country; they simply believed that a love of one's own country could not justify the hatred of another. The British government was relatively lenient to those who had objected purely on religious grounds. What irked them were the socialists, who – in approaching the question from a humanitarian rather than a religious point of view – framed their argument in anti-capitalist terms.

The Quaker position was perhaps easiest to understand

because of its long tradition of pacifism. Nevertheless, it still required fresh thinking and Beatrice and Kees were very much part of that discussion during their branch meetings of the FOR. It was time to step up the pressure and a new round of street campaigns began.

One Saturday in December, 1916 – just a few days before Christmas – Kees, who had been preaching regularly every week outside a munitions factory, took up his position as usual. A crowd of people gathered round; there were even cheers of support as Kees declared, "Love your enemies, do good to those who hate you!" and "The Germans are our brothers. Let the soldiers throw down their arms and refuse to fight and join in the brotherhood of man."

Unnoticed by Kees, two special constables were observing him and writing down everything he was saying in their notebooks.

A drunken soldier picked up a chair and shook it at Kees, accusing him of being a traitor. Undeterred, Kees carried on. He was an excellent orator and compelling to listen to. The crowd became enthusiastic, and this time the two special constables on duty intervened to stop his open-air speech, on the grounds that it was 'becoming disorderly'. Kees was moved on.

Beatrice, who was pregnant again with their fourth child, became more involved in the campaign work alongside her husband. Now that they had moved out of Helen and Charles' house, they felt free to campaign more openly in the spring of 1917. The war showed no sign of ending and in April that year the United States declared war on Germany.

Kees continued speaking in squares and on street corners, with the expectant Beatrice handing out leaflets to the crowds. For many months they escaped punishment. She would later remark to her children: 'It speaks much for English freedom of speech that Daddy was able to speak at street corners and in squares without being officially forbidden.'

Baby Julia arrived, on 12th June, 1917. Kees had been hoping for a son this time but the couple could now joke with each other, "a girl, never mind". Helen was coming up to five and Beatrice enrolled her at a nearby kindergarten for a few hours each day. Emma was two-and-a-half and Paula was eighteen months. They were sweet-looking girls, all with straight fair hair and blue eyes.

That autumn an important meeting of the Birmingham branch of the FOR, of which Kees was still Secretary, took place. It was reported that there was a strong pacifist movement growing in the Welsh mining villages. What it needed was somebody to tap into and mobilise that anti-war feeling. The ideal person was Kees, and so it was decided that the Boeke family would move to Wales for a short time so that Kees could continue his public speaking.

They reached the town of Neath in early January, 1918, on a bitterly cold afternoon. Beatrice and the children sat in the unheated and dilapidated waiting room of Neath station, while Kees went to find them somewhere to stay. His family were glad to see him return with the welcome news that he had found a suitable boarding house. Kees began to speak at church and chapel meetings but (he complained to Beatrice) the congregations were not always receptive to his message; he was thrown out of one Sunday school meeting. Their landlady became increasingly alarmed by their anti-war activities and asked the family to find alternative accommodation after just two weeks.

Kees's manner became more strident and this caused suspicion. That he was Dutch did not help — people in Wales mistook him for a German. He was summoned under a local bye-law for causing an obstruction, and arrested. He refused to pay the fine on principle and was taken to Swansea prison where, during a search, sufficient money to pay the fine was found in his pocket so he was released immediately. However, Kees was not to enjoy the freedom he had had for much longer.

The press took the opportunity to goad the police. 'How is it,' asked a Birmingham newspaper, 'that this young Dutchman is left free to undermine military authority and public morale? We answer [this question] by publishing a certificate of his marriage.' The implication was all too clear. Being married to one of the Cadbury elite meant that Kees could act with impunity.

But his time was running out. While all the family were still in Wales, Kees received a summons from the police to appear at the Birmingham Law Courts on 17th February, 1918. He was to stand trial for offences under the newly-introduced Defence of the Realm Act (DORA).

At this point, the couple were not especially perturbed by the summons. Kees had escaped serious punishment so far and although prison was a possibility the prospect of confinement held no fear – if anything, Kees and Beatrice had a romantic view of being amongst the 'suffering humanity'; the outcasts who existed marginalised on the fringes of society. There was almost a nobility to it.

The court day came round quickly. The precise charge against Kees was that, in a public square, he had '[made] statements likely to interfere with the success of His Majesty's forces and prejudice their recruiting and discipline'. Kees had decided to conduct his own defence and Beatrice sat in the gallery along with many friends and supporters from the FOR and the Society of Friends. Three specific statements were read out to the court, based on what Kees was purported to have said:

1. The Germans are our brothers.

2. Man was not made to kill man.

3. The quickest way to end war would be for all soldiers to lay down their arms.

These statements, the prosecutor argued, were clear evidence that Mr Boeke was an insurrectionary force, who posed a serious threat to the country's stability.

Hearing such a bald statement, Beatrice had the first inkling of the trouble her husband was in. The courtroom atmosphere was tense. The press waited in the gallery, pens poised to record the dramatic events. The prosecutor's face was scarlet with indignation as he raged against the audacity of this 'troublesome foreigner' who thought he had the right to 'interfere in the affairs of Great Britain'. Why, he said, he would have 'knocked Boeke off his pins' if he had heard the accused's words for himself. When the constables took the stand, one of them reported that, in fact, Mr Boeke had been speaking at an ordinary religious gathering, albeit one that looked as if it were getting out of hand.

Beatrice was called to speak. She walked calmly to the stand and stated in her soft melodious voice: "To say that the constables had saved the situation is quite to exaggerate the facts."

Kees took the stand next. He argued that the first two statements he had been reported as saying were entirely compatible with the teachings of Jesus Christ. The third statement, which called for soldiers to thrown down their arms, could not be construed as interfering with the success or discipline of His Majesty's Forces.

"If I saw a house on fire," Kees said, "and people there in danger, I should smash the windows and do other unlawful acts, if by doing so I might save the people. If I have broken one law it is only to fulfil a higher law." But, unsurprisingly, the magistrate, Lord Ilkeston, was in no mood to listen to such philosophical arguments.

He ruled that Kees should pay a fine of £50 or go to prison for 41 days. Out of principle, and because he believed he had not acted unlawfully, Kees refused to pay the fine. The result, as he had perhaps anticipated, was that he was sent to Winson Green Prison in Birmingham.

But Lord Ilkeston had something else up his sleeve. He also recommended Kees's immediate deportation back to Holland. Beatrice sat utterly stunned when she heard the words. Neither of them were prepared for that punishment. Her voice wavered as she called out "goodbye" and her husband was taken down to the cells. Kees was determined to keep his composure and was heard 'chatting pleasantly' with the warder. Such was the shock and disbelief in the courtroom that a demonstration in support of Kees broke out and Lord Ilkeston, in fury, ordered the immediate clearance of the courtroom.

Friends from the FOR were equally aghast and they rallied quickly in support of Kees's case. In March, 1918, while Kees was being held at Winson Green, the distinguished scholar and family friend, Gerard Collier, wrote to the Birmingham branch of the FOR calling upon all members to write to the Home Secretary to try and get the deportation order overturned.

In the March 1918 edition of *The New Crusader*, a magazine produced by the Christian Socialist pacifist, Wilfred Wellock, Kees's trial notes were printed, followed by an article from Gerard Collier that robustly defended Kees's actions.

Nobody, Collier began, questioned the sincerity of C. Boeke (Kees). His credentials as a teacher and his reputable and sincere character were described. He had served as a missionary, his wife was a member of a well-known family. Both were Quakers. How could he have been imprisoned just for saying the Germans were our brothers?

Another ally, Mr Maynard, was a key member of the FOR, and was one of a number of people who petitioned the Home Secretary on Kees's behalf. At the beginning of April, he received a reply from the Home Office. The news was not good:

'I am directed by the Secretary of State to inform you that he
fully considered your representation, but ... his duty [is] to make
a Deportation Order against Boeke. He will be sent to Holland
as soon as possible and the Secretary of State regrets he is
unable to alter that decision.'

Beatrice wrote to Mr Maynard from their house in Anderton Park Road, expressing thanks for writing to the Home Office. 'I had very much been hoping and longing to have Kees home again,' she said. She and the children were eventually granted a special visit to Winson Green Prison. On a freezing cold day in March, Beatrice, accompanied by Eveline Fletcher and the four girls, sat in a coffee house opposite the prison while they waited for their allotted hour with Kees. It was a tremendously stressful time for Beatrice: answering questions about Daddy from the bewildered Helen and Emma, and also considering what she would do next.

During the meeting with her husband – in the presence of a surly warden – she saw that he was bearing up. He had been treated reasonably well, and was even allowed to wear his own clothes, unlike some of the other prisoners of conscience (the term given to COs in jail). The separation became much worse when she learned Kees was to be transferred to Wormwood Scrubs Prison in London to await his deportation.

Here, conditions were much harsher. For a start, the prison diet was grim. Breakfast was a pint of thin porridge (made with water, not milk) and potatoes; bread and either bacon or beans or fish would usually be served up for the other meals. Occasionally cheese was given at supper time, but usually it was just a single slice of bread and butter. Food declared unfit to be served to the armed forces ended up on the prisoners' plates. During his time there Kees was alerted to the dire conditions and began to add prison reform to his list of causes. It seemed to him that the prison system had no purpose other than to break the will of the men.

The prisoners of conscience were particularly despised in war time. A prison chaplain from the Anglican church declared that all COs ought to be drowned. When breaking the news of the death of a CO inmate's cousin, the same chaplain reported it as brutally as possible. To Kees, these so-called men of the cloth were hypocrites, without a shred of humanity.

During his time in Wormwood Scrubs Kees discovered that he was actually suspected of being a German spy.

Meanwhile, at home in Moseley, Beatrice was in turmoil. A prison sentence, whilst unpleasant, could have been borne, but to face her husband being sent back to Holland, particularly while the war was still on, was intolerable. Who knew what dangers he would face crossing the Channel. Only four years ago, Beatrice had rejoiced in Kees going abroad – she had felt confident in God's protection. Now it was different. They had to make decisions and formulate plans, but with Kees incarcerated in London it was so difficult, almost impossible.

Prisoners at Wormwood Scrubs were given permission to write letters, solely 'for the purpose of enabling them to keep up a connection with their respectable friends and not that they be kept informed of public events'. Prisoner number 1987, aka Cornelis Boeke, was allowed to write to Beatrice. Arriving on the prison's official blue notepaper, Kees's letter was forced to adopt a formal tone with none of his usual loving endearments. He wrote of the 'various arrangements which will have to be made if the Home Office issues an order for my deportation – which according to Arnold [husband of Beatrice's sister, Edith] is a foregone conclusion'. His next letter, arriving two weeks later, was in tiny handwriting, the better to make use of all the available space.

By early April, the couple were making tentative plans. Beatrice and Helen, now aged five, would go to Holland, leaving the other three children behind in the care of the Cadbury family. (Helen, being a bright and intelligent child, could learn Dutch quickly, supposed Kees.) Emma, possibly, could go too but the two little ones, Paula and Julia, should stay in England with relatives. It is not known how far this plan was seriously considered but it was apparently rejected. Beatrice was not prepared to split the family up.

The authorities, perhaps wary of a publicity campaign, were determined to keep Kees's date for deportation a secret, thus denying Beatrice the chance to travel on the same crossing as her husband. On 9th April, 1918, she went down to London to visit Kees, only to be told by the prison warder he had been deported the previous day. It was as if the axe that had swayed so long above her head had fallen.

A few days later, she learned that Kees had disembarked quite safely at Rotterdam that evening and four hours later had reached the home of his mother in Alkmaar, who was much relieved to see her son.

But Beatrice's own relief was short-lived when she discovered it would be weeks, if not months, before she, too, could be allowed to travel to Holland. At this point she decided to move to London, staying at a hotel near Devonshire House in Piccadilly with the children and Eveline, and also the children's Auntie Geraldine, Barrow's wife. Geraldine was a great support to Beatrice during this time, and Barrow felt easier in his mind knowing that his wife was there to give moral support to his little sister.

It was not until three months later, in July 1918, that Beatrice was finally granted permission to travel under camouflage on a convoy to Holland. This was a highly risky enterprise: the convoy ship was anchored at the Thames waiting for the moment when it was judged safe to slip across the English Channel to the Hook in Holland. There were no guarantees of safety. The crossing would be perilous for her and the children, since rumours were circulating that the Germans were within touching distance of the English Channel.

It would be understandable if Beatrice felt that circumstances were now conspiring against her. Her original travel permit had expired and she had to go to the Home Office to be issued with a new one. Having secured the precious piece of paper, she was putting it in her despatch case when a gust of wind whipped it out of her hand and into the flow of traffic. She watched in dismay as the travel permit disappeared forever. She reported this calamity to the police, but they were unsympathetic. Matters became even worse when she returned to the hotel to find a message saying that the convoy ship was set to leave from Gravesend at four o'clock the following morning. If she missed this crossing, then she would have to begin the application process all over again. It could be another three months.

Meanwhile, unknown to Beatrice, Kees was travelling regularly to the Hook of Holland in hopes of meeting his wife and children off the boat, but each time as the passengers strolled onto the quay his family was nowhere to be seen.

Beatrice's nerves were almost at breaking point, but then the stroke of luck she so badly needed arrived. At eight o'clock that evening a policeman knocked on her hotel room door with a new travel permit. They had just a few hours to finish their packing, to say farewell to Eveline and to Barrow's wife, Geraldine. Then she and the girls could finally set sail for Holland. Beatrice would not think about the possibility of the ship being torpedoed.

6

House in the Woods,
1918-1920

BEFORE THEY BOARDED the ship, Beatrice's travel papers were scrutinised and hers and the children's belongings thoroughly searched. Every passenger was issued with a life-jacket. There was no doubt that their lives were in considerable danger. Whatever misgivings Beatrice may have felt about the wisdom of the voyage, these thoughts would not prevent her from stepping on to the ship that night.

It was an utterly wretched and miserable journey. Beatrice clutched one-year-old Julia to her bosom throughout, ignoring the cramp in her arms and shoulders, while the other girls were kept together by a set of long reins that Eveline had ingeniously fashioned. The three youngest, Emma, Paula and Julia, turned out to be poor sea-travellers and suffered horribly from seasickness throughout the fraught crossing. A young German girl, who – like Kees – was being deported, took pity on Beatrice and offered her help. It was a touching moment of kindness that proved, although no proof were actually needed, that ordinary Germans were not the enemy.

Later that morning, as daylight broke, the ship stopped at Rotterdam and with relief they trooped off. The longed-for family reunion was something of an anticlimax. Kees was still waiting for them in a Hook hostel. Once on dry land, Beatrice hastily sent a telegram to his mother to say that the boat had docked and they were catching the train to Alkmaar. From their carriage the girls looked out on the passing villages, with the pretty farmhouses and rotating windmills. As the train chugged along, Beatrice began to feel a profound sense of relief that they had survived the journey unscathed, and were now in a peaceful neutral land in the middle of a world still at war. After the air raids and the conflict in Birmingham and London, Holland was by comparison a sanctuary, a place of refuge where she and her family could find shelter.

Beatrice was glad to reach her mother-in-law's house. Oma had a cupboard full of toys to entertain the children and a beautiful garden-with-veranda to play in. Even the steep and winding staircase was a novelty for them, although Helen tumbled down one of the flights and had to be put to bed immediately. Eventually, Kees arrived home. The children were reunited with Daddy at last, but were disappointed to find him exhausted after cycling through a storm to reach them.

The summer of 1918 was blissful. Beatrice and Kees had been apart for four months and were more like newly-weds getting to know one another again. Alkmaar was an attractive town, especially at night-time when the streets were lit-up, unlike Birmingham with its dreadful blackout. Food was plentiful in the shops. Towards the end of August, however, Beatrice broached the subject of finding somewhere else to live in Holland. Staying with Oma was never meant to be a permanent solution, and Beatrice wanted her privacy back and to create her own family unit once more. Oma had been a dear, and wonderfully accommodating with the children, but she indulged her youngest son. Beatrice felt that if she did not instigate a move soon they would never escape.

Luckily, Kees's brother had seen an advertisement for a house being auctioned in the town of Bilthoven in the Utrecht region, about 50 miles away from Alkmaar. It was a large villa, next door to a wood. Bilthoven itself was a relatively new residential area that had sprung up around the railway station built in 1863. As Beatrice and Kees studied the particulars, they wondered if they were looking at their future home.

*

On a blazing hot day in late August, the couple and their two eldest girls went to Bilthoven to view the house. After leaving Bilthoven train station, they followed the directions down the tree-lined boulevard, Soestdijkerstraatweg, passing some pleasant but quite ordinary-looking villas. Had they made a mistake? They were beginning to feel downhearted when they turned right into Beetslaan (Beets Lane) and there, on the left-hand side, set back from the main road and up a slight hill, was a much grander villa surrounded by mature pine trees. The house was built of reddish brick, with painted timber cladding along the front elevation and it had a covered porch that would be ideal for sitting outside in finer weather. A wooden sign above the front door read 'Het Boschhuis'. Its English translation was enchanting: the house in the woods.

The couple were excited. Inside the house there were three large rooms on the ground floor and a kitchen. Upstairs, six bedroom doors led off the central landing. Two attic rooms, as well as a basement cellar, would give them plenty of storage space. Suddenly bored, Helen and Emma noticed a girl on a swing in a small park nearby. "Can we go and play with her?" they pleaded to their parents. While the children made friends, the girl's mother chatted to Beatrice and Kees about how suitable the area was for a young family: quiet, yet only ten miles away from Utrecht centre.

Almost immediately the couple began to visualise the sort of lifestyle they could create in Bilthoven. *Het Boschhuis* had charmed them both, not only as a place to bring up their girls, but also because of its potential to become a centre where people would gather for Friends' Meetings and continue their peace work. "Just imagine it," Beatrice said, "Henry Hodgkin and Friedrich Siegmund-Schultze sitting together under the trees." The couple had made up their minds and went to the auction determined to buy it. Using funds from Beatrice's inheritance, they successfully bid on the house. At last – the first real home of their own.

In September, the Boeke family moved from Alkmaar into *Het Boschhuis*. Oma's companion, Annie, moved with them to help with the children and Beatrice also employed a sixteen-year-old Mother's Help, called Bets.

Settling in proved surprisingly easy. Beatrice was determined to learn Dutch from the start and this, along with her warm-hearted manner, helped her to make friends. The day after they moved in, they held a Quaker meeting, attended by Belgian refugees living in temporary shelter in nearby Amersfoort. They had no furniture to speak of, so the meeting was conducted seated on packing boxes. The furnishings they later acquired were only the 'simplest and most necessary'. Beatrice still shuddered to remember the showy, opulent interiors of Uffculme and Tennessee; her taste was now 'stripped-down' and closer in spirit to the original Quaker notion of simplicity.

As the weeks passed Beatrice reflected that, yes, the Deportation Order had been a real blow and her separation from Kees an almost unbearable trial; but now they were together at last, reunited as a family, and in a place of safety. Helen had begun attending a small kindergarten class run by some Dutch friends and had settled down well. Annie and Bets were an asset when it came to looking after Emma, Paula and Julia. The children loved the woods and the grown-ups created a fairytale setting by stringing lanterns between the trees at night-time. Beatrice felt she had much to be thankful for.

Of course she missed her family back in Birmingham, especially Barrow and William, and her sister-in-law Geraldine; they had all been so protective of her and would still be anxious, no doubt. So, too, would Helen and Charles, who were still in America, but planning to return to English soil as soon as they could. And yet, whilst Beatrice would never have wished for her husband's ignominious expulsion from Britain, perhaps it was a blessing. At least in Holland they would be able to continue and build on the peace work they had started in England, only this time free from persecution by a narrow-minded and intolerant government. Or so she thought.

*

By autumn the end of the war looked to be in sight. Helen's sixth birthday on 11th November, 1918, brought an extra reason for the family to celebrate: news came through that the armistice had been signed between the Allies and the Germans, bringing an end to all hostilities. It had been anticipated for weeks but, even so, Beatrice could hardly believe the war was finally over.

That evening Kees cycled to Vreeburg Square in Utrecht to preach outdoors for the first time. Open-air meetings were illegal in Holland, unless prior permission had been obtained from the Mayor, yet Kees – perhaps in his over-excitement – had not applied for the mandatory licence. He took his position at a drinking fountain, began his speech and was promptly arrested, spending the rest of the evening in a cell being questioned and then released without charge. What should have been a joyous celebration of the ceasefire turned sour. Moreover, this was an early warning that the Dutch authorities would prove to be even less patient than the British.

Although Kees's vocal opposition to the war had, in England, led ultimately to his expulsion, he was the first to concede that he had enjoyed three years of relative freedom from the police. If the Cadbury connection had afforded Kees some leniency in Britain, then this would mean nothing in Holland.

Undeterred, Kees and Beatrice set about planning a conference, an idea which had come out of their weekly Quaker meetings. This took place two days after Christmas and prompted the start of a new organisation called the *Broederschap in Christus* (or the Brotherhood of Christ) formed with the noble, though somewhat ambitious, intention of uniting pacifist groups all over Holland. The aftermath of the Great War, as it had come to be known, was a time of heady idealism, coupled with a determination to make sure such a conflict would never happen again.

Beatrice and Kees had kept in contact with the affable Henry Hodgkin of the Fellowship of Reconciliation and they met up with him on a short holiday in April, 1919, in the seaside area of Noordwijk. The three of them worked on plans for another conference to be held at *Het Boschhuis*. Beatrice had half-joked about bringing Hodgkin and Friedrich Siegmund-Schultze together, but why not? They decided to make the idea a reality. That summer there was further excitement when news reached them that Eveline Fletcher's husband, Ernest, had been released from prison and that he and Eveline could come to live with them in Bilthoven.

The conference was planned for October that year. Since the signing of the Peace Treaty in April, it had become much easier to establish international contact again. With their friends, Ernest and Eveline Fletcher, who had now arrived in Bilthoven, and the support of Henry Hodgkin, Beatrice and Kees began issuing invitations to international delegates. Arrangements were made for some of the visitors to sleep at *Het Boschhuis* – the children and the Fletchers were shunted into a nearby *pension* to make room – and the rest would stay at the nearby Hotel de Leyn. Beatrice asked if the hotel could serve a daily dinner to all the delegates to spare her the trouble of cooking at home. She had just discovered she was expecting once again, with her fifth child.

To the surprise of many Bilthoven residents, a steady stream of international visitors began arriving at Bilthoven train station to begin the ten-minute walk to the Boeke house. Among the delegates were Henry Hodgkin from England, his German friend Friedrich Siegmund-Schultze from Berlin, Otto Roth from Dortmond, Leon Revoyre from Paris, Pierre Ceresole from Switzerland, all grasping one another's hands in fellowship. All were drawn together by their desire to say that war and Christianity were incompatible.

It was an exhilarating occasion: thirty-five men and women from ten different countries meeting in the name of peace. Ernest Fletcher, who had resumed his trade as a photographer, captured a group picture of all the attendees, with *Het Boschhuis* in the background. The Boeke children, including Helen, who was prettily dressed with a bow in her hair, sat proudly amongst the grown-ups.

One delegate in particular, Pierre Ceresole, had a profound influence on Kees and Beatrice. Ceresole, like Kees, had trained as an engineer. He was also a pacifist who had been prepared to go to prison for his beliefs – he had even taken the bold step of withholding his taxes in protest against government spending on arms. Ceresole was alive to hypocrisy of all forms. He had little patience for the pious men and women who gave small amounts of their money at church on a Sunday yet showed little humanity to their fellow man throughout the rest of the week. (He had been born into money, yet had given away a large proportion of his inherited wealth.)

Another delegate, the Finnish prison reformer, Mathilde Wrede, told the conference about how, against all advice, she had spent time alone in the cells of some of the most dangerous prison inmates in Finland. By offering friendship to these feared and despised men, she had found it possible to break through "the hard outer crust of hate and bitterness". Beatrice was deeply

117

moved by her testimony. "You must dig, dig, dig," Mathilde declared. "And if you dig long enough, you will find the pure gold in the heart of every man."

The outcome of the conference was a new group, named the International Fellowship of Reconciliation (IFOR). Kees and Pierre Ceresole were appointed Joint Secretaries of the group. The conference had been a huge success. The delegates parted joyfully, with heartfelt promises to meet again the following year.

Once the excitement was over, however, Beatrice realised Kees was near to collapse through nervous exhaustion. Throughout the conference his candle had burned brightly, lighting the way for others. Now his flame flickered uncertainly, and was close to being snuffed out. He desperately needed a rest-cure and where better to go than to Oma, his beloved mother in Alkmaar? He left Beatrice and the children behind in Bilthoven, much to his wife's unspoken disappointment.

His letters came frequently, although these did not reassure her particularly. She longed to have the old Kees back, yet his correspondence was full of moans and complaints. News of his brief arrest on Armistice Day had reached Alkmaar, and Kees was cross at having to endure comments from well-meaning relatives, 'giving me their opinions about obedience to law and order'.

Christmas was approaching, but Kees fretted over whether he should return to Bilthoven. Although it would be 'too much of a trek' for his wife and children to come to him in Alkmaar, at the same time his mother was dying to see the children again. Plus, Kees knew that if he stayed in Alkmaar there was no danger of being 'sucked into work' again.

Another cause of tension between the couple was that Beatrice had intervened to cancel Kees's plans for another international conference in the New Year, and he was grumpy about it. Of course, he acknowledged, he knew she was only doing it out of love, but (he told her): 'I am quite upset about it all the same.' He was deeply sensitive to the opinions of others and dreaded his 'funking it' being the subject of gossip around Bilthoven.

'Why am I such a stupid [sic] and so weak that I cannot do my work and help thee a bit all these months?' [he wrote] 'I despise myself for it.' In his next letter he continued the theme: '... I don't wish to be more effeminate than I am already anyhow. I am getting such a soft and weak old hound. Oh, why am I not a man!' His correspondence revealed the beginning of a tendency to black moods, hovering on the edge of depression.

Just four days before Christmas, Kees wrote again from Alkmaar. He was in a livelier, more positive mood; he had a new plan of action. He had written to the Dutch Queen asking for a private meeting so he could discuss whether she could help him avoid the threat of imprisonment from the authorities every time he spoke publicly. To him it was a 'quite logical' step as all prosecutions were carried out 'in the name of the Queen'.

He was also considering a tax boycott, no doubt inspired by Pierre Ceresole's action, or – before taking that radical step – at least asking the Queen if there were a way he could avoid paying tax for military purposes.

By the new year of 1920, Kees was well enough to return home to Bilthoven. Queen Wilhelmina had not responded to his requests, but never mind. The next few months became a frenzy of pamphlet-writing and speech-making, with Beatrice at her husband's side as he preached in the streets. He was an effective orator: his clear ringing voice, combined with emphatic hand gestures, meant he could capture and hold the attention of passers-by. However, Kees was breaking the law and, almost inevitably, another clash with the Dutch authorities would occur. Even if the couple half-expected punishment at some point, they were unprepared for what would happen to Beatrice. The events of that April shocked everyone, not least her relatives back home in Birmingham.

*

Kees had continued to apply to both government and local officials for permission to preach in the public squares in Utrecht. Unsurprisingly, those permit applications were rejected but Kees was not going to be thwarted. Undeterred and full of brio, he decided to ignore the decision and deliver his sermons anyway. How could preaching the Christian message of peace and the love of humanity be considered a criminal activity?

Beatrice was also keen to take part when Kees and their friend, Ernest, took to the streets of Utrecht. She would distribute pamphlets and also take her turn addressing the crowds. Now approaching her eighth month of pregnancy, she was well and full of energy. Kees stood on a box to begin his speech. A group soon gathered to listen: a shopkeeper with an idle moment, a bunch of unemployed men, women out shopping. Some laughed and made scornful comments; others began to nod their heads in agreement. Perhaps this man had a point about the evils of war and the brotherhood of man.

A policeman arrived, who quickly lost patience when Kees revealed he had no licence to speak outdoors. Kees, Beatrice and Ernest were all immediately arrested and fined. A stand-off occurred when they each refused to pay their fines. They had done nothing wrong, they argued. A week later, they were summoned to appear in court.

If Beatrice had expected the judge to be lenient to her, given her clearly visible pregnancy, she miscalculated badly. The judge sent them all to prison – Beatrice for a fortnight and Kees and Ernest for three weeks. All three were transported in a police van to Utrecht. The children, thankfully, were back home in the safe care of Eveline.

Utrecht prison housed two categories of offender, and was one of the few mixed gender gaols at the time in Holland, although this was scant consolation for Beatrice when she was kept separate from her husband. She, Kees and Ernest would serve their sentences in the Huis van Bewaring (literally 'House for Keeping') rather than the main prison wing – the Huis van Bewaring being used only for short sentences and for prisoners on remand. Here, the regime was not as strict. Prisoners were permitted to wear their own clothes, and writing materials were allowed. They could send and receive letters.

Daytime was not so bad. During waking hours, Beatrice shared a large cell with two drunken women, with whom she talked to pass the time. (Beatrice had learned enough Dutch to get by, although she was far from proficient.) Prisoners had access to a small library and Beatrice pounced gratefully on a battered collection of Charles Dickens, proceeding to read passages out loud to her probably bemused cellmates.

At night-time the women were put into separate cells for sleeping. When the cell door clanged shut and the key turned, Beatrice had to fight against claustrophobia, forcing herself to take deep breaths to try and still her thudding heart. It would not be good for the baby. The cell had a bed, a desk and a nail in the wall for hanging her clothes. The only source of fresh air was a grate on the floor but her condition made it difficult for her to crouch on all fours to reach it. Her greatest deprivation was caused by the opaque window that prevented her from looking at the sky when she woke up in the morning.

Beatrice and Kees were, by and large, model inmates, yet they each managed to irritate the wardens during their incarceration. Beatrice had a fine and powerful singing voice and she sang her favourite hymns aloud in the hope that Kees would be able to hear from his cell. 'What purpose burns within our hearts?'; 'My faith it is an oaken staff ...'; 'I feel the words of God today ...' Each one of these hymns was a source of strength to her and, she hoped, to her husband. But she was soon told to pipe down or there would be trouble.

She looked forward to the Sunday worship, not just to be uplifted spiritually, but also because she would be able to see Kees, if not speak to him. When she and the other women were escorted to the prison chapel, however, they were each shackled inside a tiny wooden cubicle with a small 'window' made of wire netting. A few minutes later, she heard the male prisoners being brought in behind her. Trapped inside the wretched box, she would be denied even a glimpse of her husband.

But then Beatrice heard Kees's familiar voice calling out in English: "Good morning, darling. How art thou?"

Her own reply was loud and clear: "Good morning, dearest, I am alright. And how art thou?"

This audacious breach of the rules infuriated the warden on duty and Beatrice and Kees were immediately sent to the Director of the prison, who reprimanded them and withdrew the privilege of attending the church service for the rest of their sentences.

Later, in his cell, Kees made sketches of the wooden boxes in the chapel and he planned to write an article about the barbaric treatment of prisoners.

The term in prison allowed Beatrice plenty of time for contemplation. Many troubled questions buzzed in her head. What would happen if the baby arrived early? Were the children alright? What would Barrow and Helen say when they heard the news of her imprisonment? As Beatrice turned all these questions over in her mind, she felt deeply frustrated that people had not yet grasped what she and Kees believed in. If only people could see her husband as she did. To the authorities he was a dangerous trouble-maker, a rabble rouser, yet to her he was passionate, with a deep faith in humanity that matched her own. She stroked her bump to comfort herself. The baby was active; every kick and movement told her that this one would be lively.

After two long weeks, Beatrice was released and then a week later – on her thirty-sixth birthday – so was Kees, and Ernest too. Kees came home to find the whole house decorated with wild flowers picked by the children, at Beatrice's instigation. Shortly afterwards, Beatrice wrote to Mr Maynard, one of the FOR members who had campaigned to try and prevent Kees's deportation from England. 'It was a strange experience,' she recalled, 'to feel that for three weeks we were so near one another, yet unable to see anything of one another.'

All things considered, Beatrice was extremely lucky. Her baby, another girl, was safely born on 6th May, 1920, just eight days after Kees's release from prison. Earlier that morning, Beatrice had gone to court to support a destitute man standing trial for stealing a bicycle, and she had been taken over by labour pains on her return. The baby arrived at 5.30pm that same day. She was named Candia, after Beatrice's paternal grandmother.

The reaction from the Cadbury family to this period in Beatrice's life was, unsurprisingly, one of complete dismay. Barrow and Geraldine had been the most anxious; they had prayed constantly for Beatrice's safety and the welfare of her unborn child. News of Beatrice's imprisonment also reached her sister, Daisy, who wrote from China in early May:

'My own precious little sister,

When I got thy letter today I felt like sitting down and having a good cry. I cannot bear to think of all thou has been through, and at this time of all times when your dear little sweetheart is so nearly expected ... I cannot help feeling so anxious for thee ... It would be very hard to leave the four dear little ones but I am so glad ... thou felt confidence in Eveline Fletcher. Thou dost not say what all the trouble was about but I suppose it was something to do with the fellowship meeting?'

A week later Daisy wrote again, after hearing the good news from Beatrice of Candia's safe arrival. 'I wonder if you will have anymore [sic] trouble about holding street meetings ...' she asked, tentatively. It was a question all of the Cadbury relatives were privately asking themselves.

*

Beatrice and Kees dismissed their spell in prison as an unfortunate hiccup and life in Bilthoven continued. Kees was still keen to host another international conference, this time on an even larger scale, but there was the problem of how to accommodate all the delegates. *Het Boschhuis* was surrounded by plenty of land so they hit upon the idea of building a purpose-built conference centre near to the house, where people from all over the world could gather in love and fellowship to thrash out a new world order.

Beatrice's legacy brought in a generous dividend income each year. She and Kees used some of this money to finance the conference centre with the same excitement that Richard Cadbury had felt when he built Uffculme. They formed a co-operative called the Utrecht Building Association (UBA) and it was a novel attempt on their part to make the wages system more democratic. The UBA builders would each be paid according to their need, rather than on a conventional rate of pay determined by their qualifications, experience, length of service, and so on. The somewhat incongruous result was that the architect, who was the most highly trained, received the lowest wages because he was a single man, whereas the two labourers, with nine and eleven children between them, were paid the most. Beatrice had balked at making the men sign a contract, but the result was that the building work for the conference centre took much longer than scheduled. But if she suspected she was being taken for a ride by the labourers, she did not appear to mind. In committing some of her fortune to the building project, it helped to salve her increasingly guilty conscience regarding money.

Ever since they had begun the peace work in Holland, Beatrice had had reason to be grateful for her Cadbury legacy. It had paid for the purchase of *Het Boschuis*, funded the IFOR conference and now the building of a conference centre, the Brotherhood House, not to mention the printing of all the campaign pamphlets.

Since arriving in Bilthoven, some of the ideas of thinkers like Pierre Ceresole were taking shape in Beatrice's mind, causing her to question more deeply how she was using her wealth. It was true that since moving here they had tried to live more simply, and she had used some of her money to support relief work, but even so their lifestyle was still a choice. It was not by necessity.

Each year Beatrice's income from share dividends was about three thousand pounds after tax. Even the most skilled factory operative at the Bournville Works did not earn more than a hundred and fifty pounds per year. To Beatrice, it seemed increasingly immoral that the world should be divided into 'haves' and 'have-nots', and that the wealthy should have control over the poor, simply by virtue of their money. In her mind she was beginning to articulate a belief that the holding of vast amounts of private capital was one of the underlying causes of the war. How could she imagine she was living the life that Jesus Christ intended, preaching a message of peace, while at the same time benefiting from an income that she had not earned? She was as tightly bound up within the fabric of the capitalist system as if she had been woven into it.

In August 1920, Beatrice and Kees booked a holiday in Switzerland. They had arranged to meet the Christian Socialist Professor Leonhard Ragaz to discuss an idea that they were formulating. The children were left behind in Eveline's care, save for Candia, whom Beatrice was still nursing. Beatrice explained to the professor that she could no longer ignore the double standard of campaigning for peace and an end to world conflict, whilst still holding on to her private capital. It was at that meeting that Beatrice, with Kees's co-operation, decided to relinquish all her shares in Cadbury.

All over Europe, thinkers and commentators were trying to work out how best to rebuild their societies in the wake of the terrible bloodshed and destruction following the Great War. It had also become fashionable during the period to divert an amount of personal wealth into charitable trusts. Donating superfluous riches enabled capitalists to feel good about themselves, but

125

Beatrice and Kees had also been influenced by the principles and actions of Pierre Ceresole who had given away his inherited shares in 1915.

*

The stage was set for Beatrice to take the most radical form of action. It was not going to be easy to give away her money. Who should the beneficiaries be? She and Kees had hosted a number of peace conferences, putting up delegates in their home and in local hotels, as well as paying the bill for travel expenses where necessary. Now perhaps it was time for these organisations to stand on their own two feet, so it was decided against putting the money in the direction of peace groups like the IFOR.

It is not known how they came up with the idea of gifting the shares to the Cadbury workers at the Bournville Works factory, but it represented idealism at its most extreme. It was beautifully simple and logical. Beatrice wanted the shares to be owned collectively by the workers, for them to decide how the dividends should be used to promote the causes of peace and internationalism, and – most of all – to give the workers power to affect company policy.

At the end of that September she wrote to the workers, via Barrow, to make her offer. But as soon as the letter reached her brother in England, Beatrice was urged, by return, to come home to discuss the matter. Could she come as quickly as possible?

Part III
The Radical Years

7

The Boeke Trust –
the Greatest Gift?

BEATRICE TRAVELLED FROM Utrecht to Rotterdam by train and then by boat to Hull, where she boarded another train bound for Birmingham New Street. The lengthy journey allowed her plenty of time for reflection and to consider how she would present her plan to her brothers and cousins serving on the Cadbury board of directors. She was not so naïve as to imagine her proposal would be accepted without question.

The message she had to communicate to them was simple: it was the capitalist system itself that lay at the root of the iniquity of war. Capitalist leaders, she would argue, used their wealth irresponsibly – they let their riches pile up and enjoyed lives of untold privilege, which in turn fed their greed and made them even hungrier for wealth and power. This behaviour increased fear and suspicion, and fuelled the strife between the 'haves' and the 'have-nots', which ultimately ended in bitter conflict. And yet the majority of ordinary people accepted their lot, being blinded by the press and fooled by government propaganda. For evidence, they need look no further than the Great War, which had been portrayed as a noble cause, yet where was the heroism in forcing men to become killing machines?

While the anti-war protests in England – before Kees's deportation – had been important, they had only been challenging the war itself instead of addressing its root causes.

Beatrice now wanted to expose the truth, which meant digging down to the roots of war and laying them bare in order to prevent the repeat of a conflict like the Great War. And yet, Beatrice would say to her brothers, the problem was that she was trapped within the capitalist system. As the daughter of one of the country's most famous capitalist enterprises, how could it be otherwise? She felt like a hypocrite. Yes, she had used her inheritance to fund the peace groups that had met in Bilthoven, but was this not just like the patronage of her father and uncle, whom others said paid lip service to good causes?

Beatrice was desperate to right this wrong. Her growing consciousness aroused guilt and a profound shame in her. Until recently, she had never even questioned her entitlement to her father's legacy. It would be important to tell her brothers that she still admired what their father and Uncle George had achieved. They had been generous to the workforce at Bournville, treating the employees almost as an extension of their own family. She had witnessed how much her father and uncle had cared for their welfare: the pleasant working conditions and leisure facilities and adult education and savings schemes. Beyond the realm of the factory, they were generous public benefactors. Hadn't her father donated his own home, Moseley Hall, to public use? When Beatrice thought back to her childhood she saw and understood the original Bournville vision. And yet ... Cadbury was a business: its goal to make a profit.

Beatrice was sure her brothers, too, harboured questions about their wealth and would understand her desire to use her legacy for the wellbeing of their fellow man. Barrow, William and Richard Junior were all generous benefactors, in their own way, just as their father had been. She knew that William, now Lord Mayor of Birmingham, had been responsive to a petition to establish a Lord Mayor's fund to help relieve the distress of children in Central Europe. Over fifteen thousand pounds had already been raised.

But, she would say, she had been reading all about Marxism and socialism, and discussing these ideas in earnest with the most influential thinkers. These new ideas had taken root inside her and disturbed her old way of living, and challenged her beliefs. She was sure her brothers meant well, but she now found their attitudes and actions just a little bit (dare she say it?) self-satisfied. But Beatrice knew she would have to be extremely careful how she worded that to her brothers.

*

A local train, which had served the Bournville factory workers since the 1880s, brought Beatrice into the station four miles south west of the city centre. Just before the train came to a stop, she glimpsed the distinctive orange and brown signs painted on the factory buildings. Bournville and Cadbury: two names synonymous with one of the best-known brands in the country.

It had been a long time since Beatrice had visited the Bournville Works. As a child it was an occasional Bank Holiday treat to visit when the factory floor was empty and the machines silent. Then, she was given a single box by her mother and permitted to fill it with as many chocolates as she could fit in.

Much had changed since those golden days of childhood.

By 1920 the company had grown from 200 employees to over 6000. Richard and George's sons no longer had quite the same fondly benevolent relationship that the original Cadbury Brothers had enjoyed with their workforce. Beatrice remembered her father saying that in the early days he had walked the young female employees to the train station each evening out of concern for their personal safety. Back then, he and her uncle had known every employee by name, but that was now impossible.

Close to the Bournville offices, on the wall of the ladies' swimming baths, a memorial had been erected bearing the names of the 200 Cadbury employees lost in the war. Birmingham had sent 150,000 men in all to fight. Of these, 11,000 were killed in action. The wall plaque poignantly reinforced what a futile and tragic waste of human life the Great War had been.

With her arguments fully rehearsed she was ready and feeling confident about facing her relatives.

*

When the Bournville Works was built in 1879, two offices for Richard and George Cadbury were built next to each other. A private passage between the two rooms enabled each man to pop to and fro whenever an urgent business matter needed resolving. Now, some forty years later, their sons were seated around the board table in what had been Richard's office, a large but cosy room lined with hand-crafted wood panelling. A welcome fire roared in the grate. The windows looked out onto a pleasant flower-bed with roses and shrubs.

It was here that Beatrice faced a formidable-looking team of directors, who each stood and beckoned her to sit down. Four men, dressed almost identically in black suits, waistcoats and crisp white shirts were present: her eldest brothers, Barrow and William; her cousin, George Cadbury Junior; and a distant relative, Walter Barrow, her solicitor, legal advisor and executor of Richard Cadbury's will back in 1899. In a tradition established by Richard and George, her brothers and cousin wore fresh flowers in their buttonholes, picked daily from blooms that grew in the Bournville Works garden.

Beatrice, by contrast, had precious little interest in appearances. At home she was happy to wander barefoot or in sandals without hosiery. When out she preferred simple and functional outfits, without any finery. Any onlooker walking past the boardroom at that moment might have thought this was a disciplinary panel between the directors and a wayward Cadbury employee about to be gently chastised for stealing chocolates from the production line, or for arriving late for work without a clean uniform.

Beatrice nodded at each of her relatives in turn: her dear brother Barrow, now fifty-eight and almost bald, with a neatly-trimmed pointed beard. He was still lean from his habit of walking and cycling everywhere at great speed; William, five years younger than Barrow, was as handsome as ever, his strong features and heavy moustache disguising his sensitive personality; George Junior, full-figured with a plump and jovial face, whose development of the Dairy Milk chocolate bar in 1905 had been staggeringly successful; and finally the sober Walter, brought in no doubt, thought Beatrice, for his expertise in company law.

*

They were all confident there would be no quarrels. That was not the way of members of The Society of Friends. Every person present at the meeting was schooled in Quakerism, and therefore used to a form of moral deliberation in which everyone played their part in the decision-making process and accepted a collective responsibility for resolving troubling matters.

Beatrice began by asking if her letter had been distributed to the Bournville workers. She was keen to know how they had reacted to the proposed gift of her Cadbury shares, although she suspected that Barrow would not have passed it on prior to this meeting. Barrow explained that certain matters about her plan needed further discussion; therefore her letter had not yet been circulated. (Barrow had, at this point, passed it to Tom Hackett, one of the worker's representatives, but Beatrice did not find this out until weeks later.)

Beatrice knew that her talk of the end of capitalism and class conflict was positively alien to the busily productive world of the Bournville Works. Her brothers, she suspected, distrusted some of the influential groups in Holland she was involved in and would find her stance threatening. She was right.

In Barrow's early years at the factory he had started right at the bottom, under the same working conditions as an ordinary employee. At no time had he felt any conflict with his fellow workers. On the contrary, he remembered his work colleagues in those early days with great affection and valued the spirit of co-operation and fellowship he experienced, detecting not the slightest animosity towards him, despite him being the founder's son.

Beatrice did not doubt his sincerity and was sure that he was using his wealth responsibly but *as a general rule* capitalism was at odds with Marxism and the 'new ideas of socialism'.

'The great war,' she had written to the Bournville employees, 'and its appalling consequences have led us to believe that the private holding of capital, such as we have done up to the present time, lies at the root of nearly all the social and economic trouble in the world today.' To Beatrice and her husband, the Great War had been but a symptom of the inequalities and social injustice in the world.

Surely her brothers could understand why she felt anxious and guilty about her Cadbury fortune and would believe her when she said this was something she had given great consideration to?

But Barrow, William, George Junior and Walter had prepared well for the meeting and the objections to her proposal stacked up against her one by one. She was about to discover that giving away her legacy would not be as easy as she had first assumed.

The first counter-argument was on purely legal terms. Beatrice's legacy was made up of two types of shares: Preference Shares and Ordinary Shares. Preference Shares were Beatrice's to do with what she liked and which she had, in fact, already sold for Russian famine relief. Ordinary Shares, on the other hand, carried voting power. They controlled the policy of the business, and could not be sold or passed on to other parties. (A further complication to the matter was that in 1919 Cadbury and its once-competitor J.S. Fry Ltd. had merged to form a new holding company, the British Cocoa and Chocolate Company, in a move to see off its rival, Rowntree's.) This restriction on Ordinary Shares prevented people other than Cadbury or Fry family members determining the future direction of the company. This condition was unlikely to be relaxed in the foreseeable future, Barrow said.

"In any case," William pointed out, unable to contain himself any longer, "It's not as though Cadbury exists purely as a machine for making money!" Beatrice ought to know that the welfare of the workers was always uppermost in their minds, just as it had been when their father and uncle had first created their blueprint for Bournville. It was a well-run factory with extremely pleasant working conditions. And what about the social housing where workers could rent a decent home and a back garden planted with fruit trees? The Bournville model village had been admired by urban planners the world over.

Privately, William thought that Beatrice was hardly being fair. He had set up a charitable fund to help relieve the distress of starving children in Central Europe. Meanwhile Barrow worked tirelessly with the Adult School movement and as a benefactor of three open-air schools for sick children. They could hardly be accused of a dereliction of their civic duty.

And at the factory only two years before the Cadbury board had agreed to set up Works' Councils to ensure a robust system of consultation with the workforce. The Bournville employees were far from being oppressed and down-trodden slaves of capitalism. On the contrary, Cadbury had some of the best working conditions of all the factories in Britain. He felt Beatrice had merely got carried away with the meetings in Bilthoven. Now she was back at home he hoped he could convince her to see sense.

Before Beatrice had time to frame her response, Barrow stepped in to make a third point. In his soft and courteous voice, he explained that the legacy had been given to Beatrice by their father not just to support herself, but to enable her to look after any children she may have.

"Your children are still young," Barrow said, thinking of his five nieces, "but you must consider their future." Whatever plans she had for her inheritance she should, he argued, set aside a number of shares (to the net value of around a thousand pounds per annum) for the children. "You want them to have proper education and training, surely?"

Then, he maintained, when her children reached the age of twenty-one, they could decide for themselves. William nodded, indicating his complete agreement. "As parents we ought to give our children the freedom to think for themselves. We ought not to decide for them matters that might profoundly affect their later life." Beatrice should allow her daughters to make their own decisions when they came of age, without depriving them of their rightful inheritance before that stage was reached.

One issue remained unspoken, but it was in the minds of all the men. Kees Boeke. If Beatrice gave away all her inheritance, what on earth were the Boekes going to live on? Her husband had not had a proper job since being forced to resign from his teaching post in 1915. With his patchy record of employment so far could Beatrice really rely on him to become the breadwinner for his wife and five children?

The afternoon was darkening. A fresh pot of tea and some sandwiches arrived. Barrow wished his sister would eat more. He knew that she and Kees had begun following a strict vegetarian diet earlier that year and her usual slender frame seemed slighter than ever. The hollows under her eyes and cheeks troubled him. Perhaps he would ask Geraldine to speak to his sister and make discreet enquiries, woman-to-woman – his wife was knowledgeable and well-informed about health matters. Beatrice could not sustain herself purely on idealism and self-righteousness.

Now it was time for George Junior to speak. He bluntly challenged Beatrice's suggestion that her shares should be given to the workers to decide what to do with. "The Works' Councils are purely for Works' purposes," he argued. They were there to deal with worker suggestions for improving factory life. George Junior could not envisage the Works' Councils being willing to administer a fund and make decisions about how the money should be used outside the Works. How would such a decision-making process operate? How would the ordinary workers be able to determine which causes the money should be spent on? It was highly impractical.

Beatrice gave the impression of having listened carefully to all these points. She promised to "seriously consider" Barrow's comments about the children's education and she would discuss the other viewpoints expressed with her husband when she returned to Holland.

By now it was late afternoon and the employees were preparing to go home for the weekend. Walter Barrow, who had been silent so far, spoke up to reiterate the legal impossibility of giving away Ordinary Shares. The men left the meeting satisfied they had successfully fought down Beatrice's proposal. They had little intuition yet of Beatrice's unrelenting sense of conviction about the matter.

*

For the duration of her visit to Birmingham, Beatrice stayed at Tennessee with her sister Helen. Her beloved husband, Charles, had recently died of a sudden stroke. The whole family was reeling from shock and Beatrice's priority immediately after the Bournville meeting was to comfort a distraught Helen. Beatrice, too, was deeply upset – Charles had been like a father to her in many ways, in the period after Emma Jane had died and before her marriage to Kees.

Two weeks later, over a morose breakfast with her grieving sister, Beatrice received a letter addressed to 'Mrs C. Boeke'. It was from a Mr Tom Hackett, the Bournville Works' foreman and the chair of the recently-created Works' Council. Beatrice scanned through the letter – it was three pages long. This was what she had been waiting for: a response from the Cadbury workers to her gift. With some satisfaction she realised that Barrow must have actually passed her letter on after their meeting, at least to one of the workers' representatives.

Tom Hackett – who was to become a key player in the discussions surrounding Beatrice's legacy – had written an extremely articulate and surprising response. Tom had been at the Bournville Works for a number of years; he was an educated man with an excellent grasp of the issues. He was well placed to speak on behalf of the workers. A cynic might suggest that the Cadbury siblings and cousin had selected the best man to respond.

The letter, dated 11th November, 1920, told Beatrice (albeit very politely) that she was making completely the wrong decision.

Tom Hackett insisted his letter should not be read as a criticism of her, but nevertheless he was very worried by the proposal she had put forward. With a lawyer's skill he outlined his case. First, he entirely agreed with her that the competitive system of industry was wrong and opposed to the ethic of Christianity, and that 'harsh and greedy practices' should be substituted with a 'kind of co-operative commonwealth'. But, where he had to *disagree* with her was about the chances of a 'revolution' bringing about this change. 'I almost tremble at the thought of Revolution,' he confessed; it would be both 'unsatisfactory and futile'. No, he argued, change must come about through evolution and by educating the common man, not by revolutionary means. He conceded that this way was slower but probably 'the only way'. Tom Hackett did not believe it was possible to change the relationship between capital and labour, warning that: '...the method of conducting the business of Cadbury Bros. Ltd. will not be altered one iota if some of the profits accruing therefrom are administered by someone other than yourselves.'

In short, Beatrice's plan was a non-starter.

Tom could confidently say he knew the mindset of the men and women who laboured in the factory day after day. He estimated that amongst the Bournville workforce as a whole 'the number in sympathy with your ideals of internationalism and pacifism are probably not more than 5% to 10% at the most'. The workforce was simply not ready to benefit from her act of generosity. 'Hence, to immediately hand over so much power to be administered by a large group of people regardless of their outlook and purpose in life seems to me to be liable to defeat the whole end you have in mind.'

He finished the letter with an appeal for her to think of her children: '... remembering also that you have your own children to educate ... you should be certain that this duty is not entirely overlooked'. His words were diplomatic but they echoed precisely what Barrow and William had said. He fully understood Beatrice 'wanted to work with a sense of greater freedom, born of consistency with your principles ...' Even so, he could not support her idea.

*

To Beatrice, this unexpected rejection of her offer was a blow. She returned to Bilthoven somewhat crestfallen. Early the following year, she wrote an equally polite reply to Tom Hackett's letter, generously thanking him for helping her to grasp the situation more clearly.

'Our great desire,' [she wrote] 'in what we wanted to do was of

course to give to the workers by handing over our shares not
only the responsibility of deciding how to spend the money,
but also a voice in the policy and management of the business.
We realise now that this is impossible as this power can only lie
in the hands of ordinary shareholders and the ordinary shares
cannot be transferred outside a limited circle.'

But, although dejected, Beatrice was not going to give up. On
29th April, 1921, she composed another lengthy letter to all the
Bournville workers.

'I should like to make it quite clear that although as a shareholder
I am signing this letter alone, it expresses the united thoughts of
my husband and myself.'

To give the letter an added gravitas, it was signed 'in the
presence of Pierre Ceresole and Ernest Fletcher'.

The letter spoke of taking a step forward. 'We have decided
to hand over the ownership of the Ordinary Shares I now possess
to you collectively.' She acknowledged the practical and legal
difficulties in transferring the Ordinary Shares, but was confident
that they, the workers, could be entrusted to make the best possible
use of the shares for the good of society.

'We feel sure,' [Beatrice wrote] 'that those who originally drew
up this arrangement did it solely in order to guarantee that the
ideals which led them to the establishment and management
of the Works should be maintained. But we also believe that if
you, as holders of these shares would be to a certain extent able
to control the Works, you would wholeheartedly co-operate in
order to make them an organisation solely for the service of the
community in the widest sense ... The question of control of
Works by the workers is the great issue of the struggling workers
the world over...'

Beatrice believed that the transition period to revolution
was nigh, and that the workers could take this step in helping to

learn to deal with the 'new and better world order' when it came, 'where surplus wealth generated by competitive industry is used by the workers to alleviate every suffering and hardship – whether that be work for peace and reconciliation to end class and racial strife and the divided society where bitterness and humanity still exist,' or work 'to alleviate the suffering caused by the capitalist order of society, work to study better methods of production and distribution, education and better ways of living.'

*

The following month, her brothers sought the advice of a Dutch lawyer, Dr Bisschop, to find out how Beatrice's children would be affected under Dutch law by her decision. His response was as hostile to Beatrice's intentions as that of the Cadbury board and Tom Hackett.

> 'I am afraid,' [Dr Bisschop declared, sardonically] 'that Mrs
> Boeke's intended disposition of her property ... might create
> trouble after her death, unless in the meantime the capitalistic
> world had come to an end or Mrs Boeke had become a member
> of a Russian or other idealistic state in which the rules as to
> property and inheritance do not count.'

He fleshed out the reasons for his objections according to Dutch law. If the Dutch laws of inheritance remained the same (as was likely, in his opinion) and Beatrice's children survived her into adulthood, then her donation to the Cadbury workers 'might be attacked [sic] by her children (or their legitimate offspring)'. In the case of there being three or more children then the amount that could be claimed was three quarters of the estate which a parent would have left at the time of his or her death if no donations to third parties had been made. In other words, the children could insist that they 'shall succeed to the legitimate share not only of all property which the parent leaves' but also 'such amount as the parent would have left had it not been given away as a donation during his or her lifetime'. It was a potential minefield.

He stated categorically:

'I cannot advise the Directors of Cadbury Limited to co-operate with Mrs Boeke in manner [sic] as contemplated by her.'

However, Dr. Bisschop *could* see a way forward for Mrs Boeke to 'attain the realisation of her lofty ideals without compromising the rights of her children'.

He suggested that she might transfer her shares under an English trust deed to English trustees to pay the income derived during her lifetime to the Cadbury workers, and 'after her death to hold the capital for her children absolutely'. He advised at least three trustees should oversee matters – one to act on Mrs Boeke's behalf, one to act on behalf of the Cadbury workers and one trustee for her children. He advised the trust be made in England under English law, as Dutch law did not recognise trusts as legal entities.

Meanwhile, at Bournville a sub-committee of the Works' Council had been formed to discuss Beatrice's offer. Dr Bisschop's report was passed on to them. In the middle of August 1921, some ten months after her initial offer, Beatrice received an unsigned letter from this sub-committee explaining their complete agreement with the Dutch lawyer's opinion.

Whilst acknowledging their 'high admiration of the lofty ideals and the spirit of self-sacrifice' and 'a very keen sense of appreciation of your generosity' the sub-committee was concerned about the position of the Boeke children. In Beatrice's original letter she had written passionately of the workers, 'not only those manual and mental workers who by their labours produce wealth, but those who do not produce wealth in the material sense... Wives and mothers whose work lies in the home, teachers and thinkers who enlighten us, etc.'

Now, the sub-committee responded:

'The Committee feel very strongly indeed that in offering to hand over the shares and their income absolutely, you are making a very much greater sacrifice that you are justified or called upon to make. They think you will admit, in fact your letter practically admits as much, that whilst you may not be directly producing wealth, at the same time you are doing good work in the world for the benefit of humanity generally, and undoubtedly you come under the heading of those who are working for the benefit of the world in general and as such you are entitled to a certain measure of support from the community.'

Beatrice ought to consider the 'proper maintenance' of herself and her husband and the 'proper maintenance and education of the children'. The letter continued:

'...whilst the Committee are not desirous in any way of flattering you, they consider that the world has everything to gain by giving to the children of parents with such lofty ideals the very best by way of maintenance and education that the community can supply, if only in order that those lofty ideals may be perpetuated.'

The letter concluded with a plea that Beatrice and Kees keep an amount of the share dividends sufficient for the family's needs and the children's education. Later, the sub-committee's stance would be pithily summed up by a newspaper headline from the *New York Times*.

CADBURY WORKERS UPSET BY GIFT: URGE DONOR
TO KEEP SOME OF IT.

*

Initially, Beatrice strongly rejected the suggestion of a legal trust and was unwilling to put her signature to such a document, claiming an objection on ideological grounds. The situation at

143

Bournville had reached an impasse. Back home in Bilthoven, life was moving in a new and extremely radical direction. Beatrice and Kees were considering a withdrawal from the Dutch state entirely. They wanted to set up their own Community Council as an alternative to the state, which was 'an institution of violence' as they saw it. They had a vision of the community council being a viable alternative to local government, with its own secretariat, its own newspaper (a community journal) and its own commitment to causes based on local needs. Utrecht was desperate for more social housing, for example; the prisons were in dire need of reform; unemployment was spiralling out of control. There were so many social problems to tackle and evils to eradicate. More books were added to the library at *Het Boschhuis* and downstairs the rooms were turned into offices as the hub of operations. The family moved their living quarters upstairs.

Beatrice was frustrated by what appeared to be a stalemate situation in Birmingham. In her opinion, the workers at Bournville had missed the point of the changes in society that she and Kees were trying to bring about. She wanted to give away her legacy and yet Tom Hackett and the other workers were encouraging her to hold on to it. This proved there was still much work to do in raising the consciousness of the workers.

Fed up and dejected, she and Kees discussed what would happen if they withdrew the offer of the shares to the Bournville workers. Perhaps *that* would trigger a change of heart.

She wrote and sent two crucial documents, the second of which had the effect of a rocket when it arrived in the hands of the sub-committee. The first letter, dated 7th April 1922, was a letter apparently from the recently-formed Bilthoven Community Council to say that Beatrice had offered ownership of the shares to the group and that it was willing to accept them. 'One of us, however, expressed the thought that the handing over should not take place without the permission of the Bournville workers.' Therefore, the Bilthoven Community Council would like to invite some of the workers' representatives over to Holland (with expenses paid) to discuss if they were really sure they did not want Beatrice's Cadbury shares.

Two weeks later, after hearing no response, Beatrice wrote to the Bournville workers with reference to her offer to the Bilthoven Community Council. She reiterated the point that if the Bournville workers were not interested in the shares then she would, with regret, hand them over to the Bilthoven Community Council. Beatrice wrote that she was sending her letter not only to the Cadbury directors and to the men's and women's Works' Councils, but also to 'one or two friends in Birmingham who might be able to help bring the whole correspondence to the notice of you all'. Again, she issued the invitation to come to Bilthoven to discuss the matter.

That was enough to stop the Bournville workers in their tracks. A letter was fired off to Beatrice on 13th May saying that Tom Hackett and Kathleen Cox (from the Women's Works Council) had agreed to travel to Holland on Friday 26th May, 1922, if it would be convenient for them to stay in Bilthoven for the weekend.

Tom Hackett and Kathleen Cox held an emergency meeting with the sub-committee at 4pm on the day before Tom and Kathleen were due to travel. Eleven men and women, including Walter Barrow, the lawyer, were present.

The notes from that meeting record that a Mr W.A.M. Beard stated, "I would rather have the money here at Bournville than in the hands of those Dutch visionaries!" He proposed a motion that the Bournville workers had a prior right to this money rather than the Bilthoven Community Council. This was immediately seconded by Mr F.J. Hoare and the motion was carried by the meeting.

They drafted a message to go out to Bilthoven: 'If you think you cannot keep it yourself, we cannot think there is anyone who has a better claim than the workers here at Bournville.'

Kathleen Cox and Tom Hackett arrived in Bilthoven the next day and had a very long conference 'lasting many hours', after which they met members of the Bilthoven Community Council (those "Dutch visionaries") who said they would be withdrawing their claim on the Cadbury shares.

The result was the creation of The Boeke Trust on 29th May, 1922, in a formal Agreement signed by Cornelis Boeke, Beatrice Boeke and Tom Hackett. The statement declared that Beatrice and Cornelis Boeke desired:

> 'That the ownership of all Ordinary and Preference Shares of the Works known as 'Cadbury Brothers, Ltd., Bournville' up till now standing in the name of Beatrice Boeke as legal owner ... be as from today transferred to the Men's and Women's Works' Council of the above-mentioned Works.'

> and

> 'That Walter Barrow [as Beatrice's attorney] from now hand over all income coming to Beatrice Boeke personally during her lifetime to the same Councils; this income consisting partly of an annuity, partly of dividends from preference shares in settlement, with in addition a small amount accruing to her for the present as one of the executors of her late mother's will.'

In addition, the Bournville Works' Council was to ensure that 'all saleable securities' (the remainder of the Preference Shares) be sold 'with all reasonable speed' and the proceeds given to Famine Relief Work in Russia.

The Boekes also told the Works' Council that they understood that in the event of Beatrice's death and providing each child was over twenty-one, then a claim *could* be made on the capital. This clause was included to mollify the Bournville workers that they were not completely depriving the children of their inheritance.

The two Bournville representatives, Tom and Kathleen, returned to Bournville and wrote a report on their visit. They had come away convinced that 'B. and C. Boeke are acting strictly on conscientious grounds' in desiring that the Bournville workers should own and administer the shares. The two representatives were somewhat in awe of what they had just witnessed. But on a sombre note they also remarked,

> '…in making this offer they [the Boekes] are bringing themselves down to a position in which a family of 8 people will have to exist on the money earned by C. Boeke, probably as a carpenter.'

The worry was still there. Kees had not yet proved his capacity to earn enough money to support his family.

Before signing the agreement, Beatrice had restated her wish that, if possible, the workers would demand a say in controlling the policy of the business at the Bournville Works. She could not let go of the original motivation for giving away her fortune.

Tom and Kathleen concluded: 'We were very much impressed by the spirit of complete self-surrender made by B. and C. Boeke and shall always feel that the ownership and use of this money is a very sacred Trust.' No doubt they were daunted by the responsibility placed on their shoulders.

Although Beatrice was unhappy at making a legal trust she hoped that the Workers could agree to be 'spiritual owners' of the Shares. The precise wording of The Boeke Trust agreement ran thus:

> 'Finally they [the Boekes] declare that they would have a conscientious objection to the making of a legal trust or agreement but that THEY CONSIDER THIS DOCUMENT AS IN HONOUR BINDING even though it may not legally be valid.'

All of Beatrice's shares were then transferred to the Men's and Women's Works' Council. The Boeke Trust accepted the responsibility for the shares that they had been given. For Beatrice there was no going back.

Following the transfer of shares there would be regular meetings of the trustees at Bournville and one of the issues they would look at carefully was the welfare of the Boeke children. Beatrice, recognising that the condition 'sprang from real affection' could not refuse the stipulation that the Boeke Trust be allowed to provide further education for the children. In fact this clause gave the Boeke Trust committee an excuse for keeping an eye on the children, particularly the educational needs of Helen and Emma, the two oldest girls.

All that remained was for the announcement to be made to the Bournville workers. There was some delay in this. Uncle George was becoming frail and on 22nd October, 1922, he passed away. Loving tributes came in from all over the world, and an account of his memorial service was given in the Bournville Works Magazine that November (Vol.XX).

In the same issue, following on from the George Cadbury tributes, there was a short article entitled 'The Boeke Trust'. It was a rather bland description of the Trust – giving no inkling of the controversies and discussions leading to its contentious formation – along with brief news of a meeting that had taken place with worker representatives of the Works' Council and Shop Committees. During the previous week, Tom Hackett had addressed a meeting to announce the Boeke Trust and to try to explain its terms. Immediately, Tom was bombarded with questions. Would Mrs Boeke's money be used to make up low wages? (Answer: no, that was not the intention.) Was the Boeke Trust committee prepared to finance a strike fund? (No.) Tom's prediction about the practical difficulties of letting the workers administer the Trust would prove correct.

Somehow the *New York Times* got wind of the story in the same month. In a scathing feature, it reported that the Cadbury workers had urged Mrs Boeke to keep some of her inheritance for her children. But, the editorial said, disapprovingly: 'she has impoverished herself and jeopardised the educational welfare of her children'.

Time would tell if this was a fair assessment.

Tom and Kathleen and other members of The Boeke Trust committee had plans of their own about how they could help Beatrice and her children. They were genuinely concerned for the welfare of the family and were determined to help, even if it meant resorting to subterfuge to do so.

8

Enemies of the State,
1923-1925

HAVING TAKEN THIS radical step of giving away her inheritance, Beatrice was determined to root out and eliminate any other 'contradictions' in her lifestyle. *Het Boschhius*, their family home, had been bought and furnished with income from her shares in Cadbury. It felt hypocritical to continue being the owner of this property. To achieve the consistency of principle she so craved, she decided to hand over the house and the conference centre next door to the public Quaker Meeting in Bilthoven. Collectively, they would all be the 'spiritual owners' of the two properties, although the Boeke family would continue to live in their 'house in the woods'.

Since Beatrice's decision in 1920 she and Kees had been preparing to live more simply in anticipation of their life without a comfortable income. They had become vegetarians, for practical as well as moral reasons. On a small piece of land they started to grow their own vegetables and the chickens they acquired gave them a regular supply of eggs. *Het Boschhius* was large and therefore costly to heat so they tried to manage with the single stove in the living room. In the winter time of 1921 the temperatures dropped so low that the coffee regularly froze in its pot. Their housekeeper at the time, Mabel Hun, despaired to find that plates piled up in the sink ready for washing were covered by a layer of ice.

Kees would also have to find a job. He was not afraid to try his hand at manual labour and for a short time he learned a trade as a carpenter. His first paid employment was at the Utrecht Building Association – the workers' collective that had built the Boekes' conference centre, the Brotherhood House, next door. It would be Kees' first paid job for six years and was based in the centre of Utrecht.

To Barrow, his brother-in-law, this was welcome news and for a short time it relieved some of his anxiety for Beatrice and the children, especially as she was expecting another baby. The experience of manual work would be good for Kees, especially as Kees had not contributed substantially to the family's income.

The harsh winter of 1921 was exacerbated by winds that gusted at 100 miles an hour across the flat Dutch plains. Each morning Beatrice stood at the door to see her husband off to work, worrying in case the raging blasts knocked him off his bicycle on the six-mile ride into the centre of Utrecht. Kees spent his days building staircases. It was tough work as the fierce winds blew through the open houses, but Kees settled well to it.

When Beatrice was in her eighth month of pregnancy she needed to lighten her load at home until the birth. The eldest girls, Helen and Emma, were sent to stay with friends in Amelo, in the eastern part of Holland. Paula and Julia were put in the safe care of their grandmother in Alkmaar. Only little Candia, now eighteen months, stayed at home to be cared for with Eveline's help. She was a bonny child with healthy rosy cheeks like her mother and curly reddish-blonde hair.

Not long after Kees began his carpentry work, Beatrice began to feel the familiar labour pains and on 21st November, 1921, the baby arrived (on Emma's seventh birthday). To Kees's supreme delight, at last it was a boy. They named him Daniel, in memory of one of Kees's brothers, who had passed away at a young age. It was a sweet moment that boded well for the future.

Beatrice and Kees were still keen to continue their public campaigning for peace. They resented the restrictions on their speaking activities, and continued to disobey the law prohibiting street preaching, each of them earning short prison sentences.

Kees, in particular, was sensitive to any implied criticism of their actions. He was keen to put an optimistic gloss on their activities and to make light of any bad news that might attract condemnation or censure from the family in Birmingham. In a letter to his brother-in-law Barrow, he wrote that Helen and Julia had caught measles (but were recovering well) and casually mentioned his wife's most recent incarceration:

'Beatrice is in prison, happily only one day. From a talk with the public prosecutor he is worried about convicting us and will give us a large measure of freedom of speech what [sic] we have been fighting for'.

The letter was signed 'with dear love, your affectionate brother'.

However, Kees was deluding himself if he thought that the Dutch authorities were in the mood to tolerate the couple, particularly as their activism was about to scale new heights.

During the many conferences in Bilthoven, the couple had been exposed to different forms and methods of political activism, one of which struck them as very valid and effective: tax resistance. They had long been unhappy at the thought of their taxes being used in part to fund the military, and Kees had already tried the novel, though unsuccessful, approach of sending his tax payment directly to the Queen with the request that it be used for charitable purposes. Sources told him that the Queen had sent the money on to the Finance Minister, where it had been absorbed into the general tax system. So this tactic was deemed a failure, and more radical action was needed.

The withholding of tax for reasons of conscience had a long history and was regarded by pacifists as a fair form of non-violent resistance. Pierre Ceresole had done it, and so would the Boekes. First, Kees wrote to Queen Wilhelmina again to say that they *were* willing to pay tax, but would withhold the amount that went to the Defence Tax for military purposes (thought to be 42%).

On hearing no response, Beatrice and Kees decided they would refuse to pay tax altogether. To begin with, reminders came through the letterbox about their outstanding tax bill. Then further demands arrived, followed by fines for non-payment, which Kees continued to ignore. Soon the Boekes' tax bill, along with the accumulated fines and added interest, came to four hundred pounds. The authorities ordered a forced sale of their assets: the date was set for 25th March 1922.

The morning of the sale was grey and drizzly. Dark clouds loomed in the sky, threatening storms at any moment. Beatrice opened the door to a sober-looking tax official with a group of bailiffs standing behind him. The local policeman accompanied the group to ensure there would be no trouble.

The tax official explained to Beatrice that they were going to take goods from the house up to the value of the sum that they owed, and then auction them off. The sale had clearly been advertised in Bilthoven because many people came, either to gawp or in the hope of getting a bargain.

Although *Het Boschhuis* was furnished in a simple manner, the bailiffs found plenty of items to remove. The children were sent upstairs to Helen's bedroom and listened, no doubt anxiously, as the house was looted.

Almost every removable item was put under auction: the tables and chairs, all the bed frames (although, with some heart, the bailiffs left the mattresses), cupboards, kitchen crockery, the books. The curtains were taken down from the windows and sold to the highest bidder. The rugs and strips of linoleum were ripped up from the floor and sold. Eveline intervened to stop the bailiffs taking the cupboard with the children's clothes and the local policeman, Berkhoff, in a surprising show of support towards the family, hid some of their silver.

Everything else was sold in the street for a pittance and the amount raised was still insufficient to clear the debt of four hundred pounds.

Worst of all, for the Boeke children watching in distress from the upstairs window, was the sight of Daddy's grand piano standing out in the street with no protection from the spattering rain. Nine-year-old Helen was particularly upset. Beatrice's engagement present to Kees, the valuable violin, also went under the hammer.

Then the bailiffs started on the Brotherhood House next door, removing the beds and any other furniture they could.

Throughout this episode Beatrice and Kees remained calm. They had the support of their friends, and God was on their side. These were only material possessions after all, they reassured themselves. The vulture-like buyers assumed that the couple would want to buy everything back again. Kees refused, much to their chagrin, and they were forced to find vans and carts to take it all away.

In a remarkable show of composure and quiet determination, Beatrice and Kees went to a public meeting in Utrecht that evening. They returned to find their friends, the Fletchers, had made the best of the situation. Eveline had tidied up *Het Boschhuis* as best she could, cleaning the stone floors from top to bottom to remove the muddy footprints made as the bailiffs had trooped through the house. She had improvised some curtains by hanging old blankets and a donated bedspread up at the windows. Beatrice was almost moved to tears to see Ernest's makeshift table, made out of a wooden trestle. An old packing box from the cellar did service as a lamp table. The children were worn out, and fast asleep upstairs as they huddled together on a shared mattress on the floor.

155

The events of the day had left the couple frustrated but more determined than ever to carry on their fight.

However, news of the auction reached the rest of the Cadbury family in Birmingham. It is not known how the news travelled there – perhaps one of their concerned friends, or an enemy acting out of spite. Whoever the source was, it resulted in a visit a few days later from Barrow and Geraldine.

Beatrice's brother and sister-in-law were astonished and upset when they arrived to find the family sitting on packing boxes, as if they had just moved into the house. Barrow insisted on buying the family some more furniture and replenishing the missing household items. This would not be the first time that Barrow and Geraldine would come to their younger sister's rescue. (Some of the Boekes' sold goods were eventually restored to them, including Kees's piano, but not all.) Barrow knew better than to rebuke his sister. He found Beatrice relentless in her idealism, yet it was more effective to offer loving sympathy rather than risk alienating her. He and Geraldine intended to keep a watchful eye over the children. They returned to Birmingham downhearted, in full expectation of more troubles of this kind.

It was against this backdrop that, two months later, the Boeke Trust was finally signed.

Meanwhile, a chill was setting in on the relationship between Beatrice and Kees and the different groups they supported. It was a major disappointment for them and a source of later disillusionment. When the next meeting of the Fellowship of Reconciliation (FOR) members was held in Bilthoven, Beatrice expected to be able to bask a little in glory for her decision to give her Cadbury shares to the Bournville workers. After all, she had taken concrete actions to spread the message of pacifism and done her bit to put right some of the inequities of capitalism. Later on, Beatrice would say of this meeting:

'We expected warm sympathy and support from its members for

giving back the capital to Bournville. Instead we met criticism and further disappointment that we had not kept it for use in furthering FOR.'

The same cooling occurred with friends and colleagues within the Brotherhood of Christ group of fellow Christians. Beatrice noted, sadly:

'We felt a slight estrangement creeping in and were drawn more to seek friends among those who did not call themselves Christians but who sought to shape their lives on purely humanitarian principles. We drew away from the Brotherhood (or they from us!)'

This period marked a shift from the Christian-based groups such as the FOR and the Brotherhood of Christ. Instead, Beatrice and Kees wanted to be aligned with those who believed in humanitarianism first and foremost. In a move that shocked the Birmingham relatives as well as the Dutch Quakers, Beatrice and Kees announced their resignation from the Society of Friends.

There were other falling-outs over practical as well as ideological matters. Since the first FOR conference in 1919, their good friend and colleague, Pierre Ceresole, had been working with the Swiss government to establish a formal alternative to National Service in his home country. He advocated a form of volunteer work where people from different countries could work together on reconstruction projects to try and repair war-damaged areas. His first project, in 1920, had been organising volunteers to rebuild Esnes, a war-torn town on the French-German border, and later these ideas would come to fruition as the Service Civil International (SCI). While Beatrice and Kees had applauded Ceresole's vision, they thought the volunteering project should be run purely on a voluntary basis rather than being formally sanctioned by the Swiss state. Ceresole left his role as Joint Secretary of the international wing of the FOR in Bilthoven, tactfully citing his commitment to other projects. The headquarters of IFOR moved to London.

In May, 1922, in the same month that the Boeke Trust was signed, Kees wrote a pamphlet called 'Break with the State', a manifesto for living which advocated a refusal to recognise state authority and a non-violent resistance to all state activities. The state, Kees maintained, was a personification of centralised violence. This was their boldest most uncompromising move yet.

From now on, they would pay no tax nor complete a tax return; Kees would do no military service; they would make no contributions to pensions or insurance for old age; they would surrender their passports, as they refused to recognise national boundaries, which they viewed as inherently divisive. They would use neither the railways nor the postal service, seeing as both were state-owned institutions.

In return, to avoid any accusations of hypocrisy, they renounced any claim for help from the police or the army. Ernest and Eveline, also caught up with this idealism, were deported for refusing to renew their now-expired passports and forced to return to England.

Beatrice and Kees saw themselves as building a new and exciting alternative society, one that would begin in the local community and spread outwards. A central part of their vision was the community journal delivered to all the households in Bilthoven. It featured a lively mix of editorial pieces, written mainly by Kees, on key issues such as peace, better housing, prison reform and the treatment of mentally ill patients in hospitals. Its aim was to encourage people to give love and service to others, rather than being driven by fear or forces or other negative impulses. Where they led they hoped others would follow. A new peace group was formed called PACO (esperanto for peace). Wilfred Wellock, one of the pacifist visitors to Bilthoven during this time, remarked in the *New Crusader* journal that he had witnessed:

'a perfect example of what two or three people might do to promote social revolution ... a glimpse of a new world where the spirit of universal brotherhood reigned.'

On 1st August, 1922, a Peace rally was held in Utrecht to mark the anniversary of the start of the Great War. Beatrice and Kees marched amongst a thronging crowd, with placards reading, 'Love Your Enemies'. Musically-gifted Kees had been busy composing his own protest songs, one of which he sang to the protesters:

"Disciples of Jesus, the times are evil

Our people distressed, our country in peril;

Our rulers are heathen, our leaders blind;

Hold fast to your Saviour; the End is at hand

Disciples of Jesus, your Master obey,

Out of pure love throw your weapons away;

Refuse to shed blood, to draw sword or kill

No land is defended by murder from ill"

But the situation became heated and there were clashes with the police, who threatened to use truncheons if the crowd did not disperse.

One evening at home, Beatrice and Kees talked about his work as a carpenter. Kees felt he should give up the job because he was depriving a real workman of the job. (In truth, the work was tough and the conditions were not particularly amenable to Kees.) Instead, he decided he would give violin and English lessons, which he could do from the relative comfort of their home.

Now that they no longer believed in owning property, the couple instigated an open-door policy at *Het Boschhuis*. Their fellow man should be free to come and go. The door locks were removed. They told themselves that this was the practical application of their passionate faith in the goodness of humanity.

To outsiders, this was a naïve and stupidly risky gamble. The outsiders were proved right when things began to go missing from their home. Beatrice, Kees, or one of the children, would wake to find that items of furniture – a cupboard or a lamp stand – had been taken. More alarmingly, items of food from the kitchen would disappear – a few eggs or a jug of cream. The children's bikes and clothes were next. They began to wonder if it was a deliberate campaign to annoy them and force them to call the police. This they would never do, seeing it as the height of hypocrisy given that they had declared war on the state and had willingly forfeited any rights to police protection.

The couple would deal with the intruders in their own way. They decided to take it in turns to keep watch each night – Kees stayed awake for the first half and then Beatrice for the other.

When her shift came, Beatrice sat at the top of the stairs. Fearful of confronting any burglar herself, she had tied a piece of string around her husband's foot so she could wake him by yanking the string if necessary. To her distress, the front door creaked open and then she heard the footsteps of an intruder creeping along the hallway. The cellar door opened – this was where some of the family's food stores were kept.

Beatrice pulled the string to wake Kees and also shouted out in shock. Kees hastily pulled on his dressing gown and raced downstairs to find the intruder running away down the path. Beatrice called out, "Come back! We're your friends! Don't run away!" The man stopped, undoubtedly confused by this response, and allowed himself to be led back into the house by Kees. In the kitchen Beatrice made him some coffee and gave him something to eat. During their conversation the man admitted to being a factory worker from a nearby town. Kees's reaction was typical: "You must be hard up, or you wouldn't come and take our things like that," he said, sympathetically.

They spoke long into the night and parted on good terms.

After that episode there were no further night-time intruders, but Beatrice and Kees – and their children – had been lucky.

*

The Boeke Trust members, who were meeting regularly for committee meetings, became increasingly concerned for the welfare of the Boeke family. Barrow had taken the step of recommending that his daughter, Dorothy Cadbury, should serve on the Trust's committee alongside Tom Hackett, Kathleen Cox and the others. (Dorothy was a down-to-earth and caring woman, who had worked on the shop floor at the Bournville Works during the war – she would be a vital link for Barrow.) The Boeke Trust began to act like social workers; they were anxious for reports from Bilthoven and wrote letters to Beatrice, who reassured them that all was well and that there was no need for concern.

What Beatrice did not know was that from the signing of the Boeke Trust agreement in May 1922, the committee members had been engaged in a subterfuge designed to protect the Boeke children from what the Trust saw as the irresponsible way of living of their parents.

Before Kathleen and Tom had left Bilthoven, they had spoken in secret to some of Beatrice and Kees's Dutch friends about keeping an eye on the Boeke family, especially now that their future income was decidedly precarious. The trust wanted to provide a safety net, albeit one that would be invisible to Beatrice and Kees.

Two of the couple's friends, Mrs Moojen and Carl Lawaetz from the Brotherhood House, had been persuaded – with some reluctance – to accept money from the Boeke Trust to be surreptitiously used to provide for the family's needs.

In the months directly following Beatrice's surrender of her legacy to the Boeke Trust, small parcels of food began to appear on the doorstep or in the kitchen cupboards. (Thanks to their open-door policy it was easy to secrete small items into the house). The milkman insisted on leaving milk and the baker a loaf of bread, even though Beatrice had stopped paying for these deliveries. She did not question the source of these gifts, but assumed that her friends had, of their own volition and kindness, grouped together to ensure the family's basic needs were met.

She had no idea that these friends were working in collusion with the Boeke Trust committee. But being a secret helper placed a burden on the consciences of all those involved. Mrs Moorjen, in particular, found it increasingly difficult to maintain the pretence and after a few months she wrote a despairing letter to the Boeke Trust Committee. She had been admitted to hospital suffering from nervous exhaustion. The doctor, Mrs Moorjen explained in her letter, had declared the cause of her illness to be having 'overworked myself'. She had been advised to stay in hospital for a month and 'then go to Switzerland to remain there absolutely alone in the mountains for two or three months.' However, she was lying in her hospital bed, unable to relax for fear of letting her friend 'Betty' down.

'… the necessity to help Betty is bigger than ever. I know I have not one hundredth of Betty's spiritual strength, but then she works a hundred times harder than I ever did.'

She continued:

'God forgive me if I am doing wrong in not telling Betty that from now it is not we who are helping her but her friends at Bournville.'

She wrote of her 'heavy heart' about having to keep the truth from Beatrice that she, Mrs Moorjen, was compromising her friend's ideological stance.

'I hope, I hope, I am not wrong in doing it like this. My feeling is that if Betty has the humility to accept my help she would be absolutely willing to accept your help, if it did not make people *misunderstand her act of giving away her fortune.'*

Deep down, Mrs Moorjen probably knew that Beatrice's commitment to her principles meant she would never agree. It was one thing for Beatrice to accept gifts from their friends, but the thought of receiving money directly from the legacy she had just given away would have been an anathema to her.

The Boeke Trust had offered to pay Mrs Moojen directly to compensate her for the money she had spent on the Boekes. But she felt uneasy about this. 'Won't you think it best if every month I write to you what [sic] Betty allowed us to do for her and that you send back to me the amount of it or part of the amount whatever you think is right to do?' Mrs Moorjen explained the sort of help that had been given to the family; this included a sewing woman (once a week at 3 guilders a time for five weeks, in order to make clothes for the children), a charwoman three times a week, and some basic foodstuffs like a bottle of cream and two packets of Ovaltine. Beatrice presumably thought these women were volunteering their time to support her in the cause.

Mrs Moorjen signed off her letter with the following words:

'It is difficult and humiliating for me to give over to you a task
that has been such a privilege to us – the help for Beatrice
Cadbury. She stands so high to us – she gives us strength in
difficult moments only by looking at her life.'

Her final request was for the postal address of Helen Alexander, Beatrice's sister, because she wanted to suggest 'some necessary Christmas presents for Betty'. It was a heartfelt letter that spoke volumes about her respect for Beatrice but also the emotional hardship the Boekes inadvertently caused some of their friends. Although Beatrice had relieved herself of the burden of her inheritance, the Boeke family were now dependent on their friends to help and support them.

The period between 1923 and 1925 would be characterised by ever-increasing battles with the Dutch authorities, where Beatrice and Kees took their idealism to an extreme (and some said ludicrous) position.

Meanwhile, the Birmingham contingent was worried about the circumstances at *Het Boschhuis*. On March 27th, 1923, Beatrice had given birth to another girl, named Theodora. The couple now had seven children – a large family by any standards but it was a particular concern, given their extremely limited financial means. Beatrice was now approaching forty and the ravages of time and prolific childbirth had taken their toll on her physical appearance. She was still desperately thin and by now her brown hair was entirely white, contributing to the impression that she was much older than Kees, although they were in fact the same age. And yet she was still driven by idealistic fervour and her energy never seemed to flag — certainly not for the many meetings and events that she attended at her husband's side, while the children were left in the care of their friends and helpers.

The couple began to question the whole nature of money – its function in society, how it corrupted people, and so on. They wondered, could they manage to live without money? The idea was appealing; they had become almost self-sufficient. In their minds, they saw themselves as leading by Christian example, creating a new and caring community unity where each neighbour would provide for the other, without the need for money to change hands.

On 6th August, 1923, Kees made a bold decision: he vowed he would no longer use money. He would not touch it. To begin with, this did not affect the family too much. Kees was still giving violin and English lessons and rather than receiving the money himself, Beatrice collected it on his behalf, which went to support their growing family, albeit in a modest way.

Their stance attracted derision and suspicion from many quarters. The police saw the Boekes as dangerous radicals and infiltrated the Bilthoven Community Council by planting a spy into a job in their office inside the Brotherhood House. The spy therefore had access to all the activities of the Bilthoven Community Council. When the man confessed to Kees and Beatrice that he could no longer keep up the pretence they went together to the police commissioner to confront him. He was dismissive, saying, "Mr Boeke, we have many more who are working for us."

The problem was also that the couple attracted their fair share of fanatics and deluded romantics as well as sincere activists. Kees, in particular, had such a persuasive manner that he perhaps did not realise the force of his words. At times they attracted passionate types who would sometimes tip over into violence.

*

In 1923 members of the Boeke Trust were due to make another visit. Beatrice invited them to stay in Bilthoven that July to take part in a conference they had been planning. (Beatrice accepted a donation of £50 from the Boeke Trust to help fund the gathering, which was in the name of peace and international cooperation.) Each time the visitors came from England, Beatrice undoubtedly felt under pressure to put on a good show, to prove that her decision to give away her fortune had been the right one. It was as if her whole lifestyle was on trial. Beatrice and the five oldest girls – Helen, Emma, Paula, Julia and Candia – went to Bilthoven station to meet their guests, Tom Hackett and Kathleen Cox. Daniel, who was not as strong as his sisters health-wise, stayed at home. After the three-day conference, the Boeke children acted out a little play for the visitors which they had rehearsed, with their parents' help.

The four eldest girls were, by this time, enrolled in the Montessori school and their parents reported they were pleased with the progress the children were making. Beatrice and Kees strongly approved of the ideas and learning methods of the Montessori school.

During their visit, the Boeke Trust members showered the children with gifts. Beatrice, although unhappy at such extravagance, knew it would be churlish to object and she accepted the presents with good grace. As well as a trip into Utrecht to get the children kitted out in clothes and shoes, Tom and Kathleen had bought fountain pens and ink, pencils and scribbling blocks, and a bike and a workbox, as well as some tennis racquets and balls. The look of delight on the children's faces was marvellous. Kathleen also broached another matter. Would Beatrice allow the Trust to pay for a family seaside holiday in Holland? The Boeke Trust had discussed this at a previous meeting and wanted to contribute the sum of £25. Beatrice balked at this but, as Kathleen pointed out, the Trust members felt that as her legacy was being used in part to fund a children's holiday home for the underprivileged, it did not seem fair that Beatrice's own children should miss out.

Tom and Kathleen went home to Birmingham reassured that all was satisfactory, if unconventional. They reported: 'Mr and Mrs Boeke and all the children looked extremely well and happy'. The following month, Beatrice wrote to ask the committee politely not to spend any further money on the family or buy them such generous gifts. After all, they had everything they needed and she disapproved of superfluous spending.

But the Boeke Trust committee continued to be concerned about the welfare of the Boeke children. Every meeting started with the same agenda item: 'Care of the Boeke Family'.

The older girls were growing up now. Helen, the vibrant fun-loving child, interested in everything and everyone, was now approaching thirteen. She had told Kathleen Cox that she intended to go to the Montessori School for at least two more years. Emma, almost eleven, was much quieter. Paula, eight, was already showing signs of being an excellent pianist, while seven-year-old Julia was a kindly, loving and intelligent girl, who wanted to be a doctor when she grew up. Curly-haired Candia, the fifth child, aged four, was clever and could occasionally be obstreperous. Daniel, the only son, was especially favoured although, like all parents, Beatrice and Kees denied this. He showed signs of being a free spirit, at one with nature, who from an early age loved to be out roaming the countryside.

The secret supply of money from the Trust to friends of the Boekes continued with the help of a new family friend, Julius ter Beek, whose intervention ensured that the delivery of food and other supplies carried on. Meanwhile, Beatrice was beginning to suspect that some covert operation was at work. In September, 1923, she wrote to the Trust in a letter that was hand-delivered by Julius, who was attending an international peace conference at Fircroft in Birmingham, funded by the Boeke Trust. Since Beatrice and Kees had repudiated the use of stamps they took the opportunity to ask their friend to take the letter in person. Beatrice was not able to attend the conference herself because she and Kees had given up their passports.

'Dear Friends, [she wrote] we are glad to have this opportunity through our friend Julius ter Beek to send you our warm greetings and best wishes for the success of your conference.

We both should have been glad to be with you, but this was quite impossible.

While we are writing we would like to take the opportunity to mention a personal matter to you.

It sometimes happens, that people here in Holland sneeringly say, that our life is a farce; for, they say, we are still living from the interest of Bournville shares. Now we do not in fact know how we are living since we have given up the use of money. But you will understand how much we hope there has been no truth in the above saying.'

Here, then, was Beatrice's first explicit acknowledgement of her suspicions that the Boeke Trust may have been directly involved in supporting her family financially. She issued a severe reminder to the Boeke Trust committee members that she expressly did not want the money to be spent on her or her family.

> 'Of course, [she continued] we do not in any way wish to dictate to you how you are to spend the income of the shares we gave over to you. But you will understand how important it is to us that nothing of it is spent on our behalf, as otherwise our witness here would be seriously interfered with.
>
> With loving greetings to you all.
>
> Beatrice C. Boeke
> Kees Boeke'

Up to now, she and Kees had operated a policy almost of wilful blindness to the matter of who was paying for the food deliveries. Beatrice had had an absolute belief – as written in scripture – that God would provide, and to begin with she had not sought to question the practical matter of who, precisely, was providing their daily bread. It did not sit well with her when she suspected that the Boeke Trust was in some way undermining her position.

At the same meeting where Beatrice's letter was relayed to the Trust, the 'lady members' of the committee were authorised to spend up to £20 to purchase warm winter clothing for the Boeke family.

*

In 1924 Beatrice and Kees initiated a series of meetings in Utrecht to discuss an important issue: 'The Sword or the Cross'. Based probably on a commentary from the American Christian pacifist, Kirby Page, the meetings were intended to provoke discussion once more about what the true Christian response to war and aggression between countries should be. To Kees and Beatrice's minds, the established church had done little to try and avert the

Great War of 1914-18, and furthermore, now the war had been over for six years, the issue of peace and reconciliation seemed to be slipping further from public consciousness. It was an issue of state authority (which often sanctioned war, violence and brutality, hence the sword) versus a life of love and service in the name of Jesus Christ, symbolised by the cross.

But the Boekes were becoming increasingly isolated. Attendance at their conferences and meetings began to tail off and the authorities were in a mood to crack down hard. Kees had still not managed to obtain permission to preach in the streets and now he was forbidden from organising meetings in the Public Halls.

Further battles occurred in 1924. In May, Kees was pleased to have been invited to speak at a meeting of the Syndicalists, but the police had threatened to close the meeting if he took part. This was particularly galling as he had found out that a leading communist had been granted permission to speak, so why not him? He and Beatrice went as attendees. At the end of the meeting Beatrice stood up and announced to the assembled audience: "My husband will now speak outside. Please be sure to stay and listen."

Kees began to speak and soon a crowd gathered in the still-warm air. Not unexpectedly, a policeman came along and tapped him on the shoulder. Usually, Kees would have defended his actions and tried to persuade the policeman he was doing no wrong, but this time he had a new tactic to try out. He made himself go limp, whereupon he fell to the ground and continued preaching from a horizontal position to the amusement of the crowd.

The policeman and his hastily-summoned colleague attempted to lift Kees and carry him to the station. But Kees was tall and although wiry, his devotion to daily exercise kept his body well-toned. It was impossible to shift him – he was a dead weight. The policemen had no choice but to leave him there. They felt humiliated in front of the crowd and would not forgive him for that.

Beatrice and Kees had an unquestioned certainty about their actions. They had right on their side because they were following what was written in scripture. What they failed to appreciate was how much they infuriated people with their pious demeanour. They were a continual thorn in the side of the Dutch authorities.

A week after that incident, Kees and Betty began speaking in one of the squares in Utrecht – again without permission. They based their text on the Sermon on the Mount (the key biblical text for many pacifists). "Blessed are the meek for they shall inherit the earth," Kees reminded his audience. This time they had no trouble from the police, so, somewhat emboldened, they decided to make their public speaking a regular feature every Thursday evening at seven. The following week a policeman appeared immediately Kees had begun his speech.

"You don't have permission to speak," he said.

"Don't interrupt me," Kees replied, "Can't you hear I'm preaching the gospel?" and he carried on, while the crowd of onlookers began to laugh. Somewhat flummoxed, the police officer went away to gather more colleagues. On their return, Kees fell to the ground as he had before, like a child refusing to co-operate with his mother. The policemen tried to haul him to his feet but could drag him no further than a few yards.

One of the policeman had the idea of getting Kees onto a two-wheeled handcart to make it easier to transport him to the station. They managed to lift Kees onto it, but as the cart only had two wheels it was difficult to balance with Kees at one end. They commandeered a young boy to sit in the other end to act as a counterweight. The crowd jeered at the spectacle they made.

Meanwhile, Beatrice took the opportunity to seize her husband's place and to continue preaching from Matthew's Gospel. Her melodious voice grew strong as she reinforced her key biblical message – to love the Lord with all one's heart

and soul and mind, and to love one's neighbours as oneself. She
needed no notes: the words of scripture came easily as she knew
them by heart.

Having deposited Kees in jail, the policeman came back and
arrested Beatrice, quickly removing her on the same handcart.
But it seemed that the biblical message had engaged some of the
crowd. (Either that, or the crowd saw the chance for some sport.)
A local carpenter stood up next to carry on the message. He was
carted off, and then an old lady began to give her testimony. She,
too, was arrested. And so it continued.

Beatrice and Kees heard later that the peaceful mood of the
meeting turned nasty and the police used their truncheons to
clear the crowds and empty the square. The couple and the other
people arrested were held at the police station until late in the
evening before being released. Beatrice and Kees cycled home
back to Bilthoven, much to the relief of their children.

Although they had planned to speak every Thursday, their
experience in Utrecht that night made them reconsider. Kees
began to slip into another of his downward spirals. He was
depressed and downhearted at the lack of progress they had
made in translating talk and ideals into practical change. Beatrice's
calm and cheerful demeanour kept her husband going through
the darker days of frustration. She provided him with a core of
wifely support, which bolstered him. A year after Kees decided
to give up the use of money, Beatrice decided to follow in her
husband's footsteps and make the same bold commitment.

But she knew they had many detractors. Sympathy for their
idealistic way of living had waned, and they seemed to have more
enemies than friends — people who dismissed them as cranks, or
others who delighted in pointing out the inconsistencies in their
'Break with the State' manifesto. One accusation of hypocrisy
stung the always-sensitive Kees particularly badly. He had used the
journal of the Bilthoven Community Council as his main vehicle
for spreading their message about the new society they were

building. The journal was sent to many Bilthoven households. Kees had publicly declared his objection to using the postal service but, as a critic pointed out, he was willing to let someone else put the stamp on for him. Upset and wounded, he gave up writing in the journal and it folded. There was now no valuable outlet for advertising meetings or staying in contact with others. Life gradually became more insular for the couple. Because of their commitment not to use the trains, the further they could travel was into Utrecht by bicycle.

The peace groups they had hosted in the heady and optimistic days of 1919 to 1921 were now flourishing outside of Bilthoven. The IFOR moved its headquarters to London; Pierre Ceresole had successfully set up Service Civile Internationale (SCI) in Switzerland; PACO became War Resisters' International and also moved to London. The world was moving on without them.

But the next phase of the Boekes' attempts to change society for the better was beckoning – and that was in the field of education.

9

Daddy Starts a School,
1926

KEES AND BEATRICE were ideologically predisposed to be interested in education. Building a new society was slow and frustrating, and they believed, intuitively, that education from a young age was the only hope of achieving harmony and peace in the world. In 1926, Kees started a home school for their children, yet the impetus for doing so actually came about through a more prosaic reason: it was an indirect result of their 'Break with the State' campaign.

Another storm had been quietly brewing for the Boekes throughout 1925, this time regarding the children's education. The children had been attending the Montessori School in Bilthoven. Based on the educational principles of the Italian educationalist and humanitarian, Maria Montessori, the Bilthoven school had been built four years previously.

The school was located in Rembrandt Square, about five minutes away on foot from *Het Boschhuis*, in a wooded setting next door to a park. The ethos of the school was based on the belief that children were individuals who learned in different ways and at different rates and with differing capabilities. What all children had in common was an insatiable desire to explore and experiment. Their desire to learn was innate. Therefore, the role of the teacher was to be supportive but to let the child learn in their own free way.

The principles of the Montessori School chimed very much with those of Beatrice. She felt a strong affinity with the Montessori style of teaching, not least because of the striking similarity to her own early educational experience at the Fröebel Kindergarten in Birmingham, which she had attended between the ages of seven and eleven.

Here, Beatrice had had a very practical and individualised introduction to learning based on the ideals of another educational pioneer, Friedrich Fröebel. When she looked back to her own childhood, she appreciated the concept of the kindergarten where children could be active, not passive, and learn through creative activities rather than over-prescription. Although there were some differences in practical application between Fröebel and Montessori schools, Beatrice instantly recognised in the Montessori school many similarities to her own schooling. Naturally, this would be perfect for her children.

When the school was originally set up in Bilthoven, Kees had served on the governing committee. Beatrice had given some financial support from her legacy, which partially funded a second nursery building for three- and four-year-olds. All of the Boeke children attended the Montessori School for a time; first Emma and Paula, then Julia, and also Helen, the eldest, who had been taught by friends of the couple when they first arrived in Bilthoven. Candia and Daniel began in the new wing and Theodora joined, too, when she was three.

Although it was a fee-paying school, the Boeke children did not pay any subscriptions. The Head knew that the Boeke family had very little money coming in, and, when the children's parents declared they were no longer using money for conscientious reasons, the fees were waived entirely in acknowledgement of Beatrice and Kees's earlier support. The Head Teacher liked the Boeke children and was keen to keep them at the school.

But then a change came about in national school funding regulations which forced yet another ideological crisis, and led Beatrice and Kees to remove their children from the school, in spite of being happy with the education they were receiving. In 1925 a new law was passed in Holland stating all school fees were to be collected by the local authority in the form of a 'school tax', rather than being paid directly to the school. At this stage, the couple were still adhering to their tax boycott. To begin with, the head of the school tried to hide this change in the regulations from the Boekes (anticipating how they would respond) but when Beatrice and Kees found out, they decided to remove their children from the school. To them, this action was completely consistent with their aim of breaking with the state.

The Head tried to persuade them to stay and managed to convince Beatrice that Candia, aged five, and four-year old Daniel, should stay for a few months longer in the nursery wing. But Kees came up with a bold yet completely logical solution for the older girls: he would educate them himself at home.

It had been fourteen years since Kees's time as head of Brummana High School in Syria, and ten years since his last teaching position at the private school in Birmingham, (from which he had been forced to resign for preaching pacifism). Both posts had turned out to be short-lived, and his teaching experience was limited, but Kees nevertheless saw home schooling as the only way forward.

Beatrice had been worried about her husband for many months. He was intensely frustrated by their lack of progress and since the 'Break with the State' campaign, his world had inevitably narrowed. He had become withdrawn and introverted, and disillusionment with other people had set in. He knew he had the power to stir up crowds as well as any evangelistic preacher;

he had seen the reactions in the eyes of the audience, the nodding of heads and the shouts of encouragement, but it was too short-lived. Kees had no idea how to harness that emotional reaction and channel it into long-term commitment to effect a real change in society. Later, he would write: 'Talking never does much good, particularly in emotional surroundings, where the immediate result may be excellent but a reaction in the opposite direction sets in later.' Beatrice, as always, kept him going and she encouraged this new educational venture, believing it would do her husband good.

"My Daddy's going to start a school," Julia was heard proudly telling her school friends one day in November. "I have an exercise book and a pencil." She, along with her older sisters, knew there was some kind of trouble at the Montessori School but the reasons would not have been clear to the seven-year-old. Julia was sad to say goodbye to her friends but to be taught at home by Daddy was like a dream come true. Like her sisters, she had missed Daddy's presence at home during the busy days of meetings and conferences and rallies, and was looking forward to having his full attention for once.

The start date was marked in the calendar – 6th January, 1926 – and the children counted down the weeks. It was decided that *Het Boschhuis* would not be suitable. There were too many comings and goings. A family friend, Mrs Kerdijk, offered the use of a spare room in her house in the Van der Helstlaan, which was just a short distance from the Montessori School and ten minutes' walk from home. There was great excitement on the first day as the four girls – Helen, Emma, Paula and Julia – marched with their father to their new school, with their exercise books under their arms and pencils on a string around their necks.

Kees had managed to procure some school desks and each daughter had their own space to work at in their new classroom. He would later admit that he was starting totally from scratch, relying on instinct rather than formal pedagogical methods. But after a few weeks of teaching his daughters, something magical happened to lift him out of his depression. Instead of trying to get his children to bend to his will, he approached his teaching in an attitude of humble surrender, trying to make himself a catalyst for learning rather than forcing learning to take place. The girls were asked to select the topics that they wanted to study. He was there to help the children develop, listening carefully to what they had told him about their interests. A month later, two friends of the children joined the home school. Additional help came from one of the Montessori teachers, who offered her services as a back-up to the work Kees was doing. The home school had got off to a surprisingly good start.

*

Back in Birmingham, the Boeke Trust committee was still concerned about the education being provided to Beatrice's children. One of the clauses in the original document signed by Beatrice and Kees had been the right of the Boeke Trust to pay for their children's further education. When committee members had visited Bilthoven in 1925 they said they would like to pay for Helen's schooling, proposing a boarding school near to her grandmother's house in Alkmaar. However, the committee had heard no more from Beatrice about this matter. In the minutes of a meeting in February 1926 under the item, 'Care of the Boeke Family', it was noted that:

> '[The Trust's] Secretaries were further instructed to enquire
> whether Helen Boeke was attending the boarding school at
> Alkmaar, and also the position of the second girl [Emma] ...'

So, when news reached Birmingham that Helen and Emma, and their two younger sisters, were no longer attending the Montessori School and instead were being taught by Kees, with the assistance of one of the Montessori teachers, they were deeply perturbed.

Mr Boeke was an engineer by training. What did he actually know about teaching? Could such an unconventional man really be trusted with the educational welfare of his children, whose ages ranged from seven to thirteen? The committee members were unanimous that they would have to find out more.

There was considerable relief when the Committee received news that William Cadbury, Beatrice's second eldest brother, was planning to visit Bilthoven for himself. He had concerns for his sister, too, and was going to take a break from the Bournville Works to see what was going on.

In the meantime, there were even more urgent financial matters for the Trust to attend to. Beatrice's friend, Julius ter Beek, had continued his secret liaison with the Boeke Trust members, feeding back detailed information about the parlous state of the Boeke household in Bilthoven and their precarious financial position.

Kees had received three Final Notices for income tax for the years 1923, 1924 and 1925. He continued to ignore them and still refused to pay the outstanding – and rapidly accumulating – tax bill as part of their campaign against the state. The Boeke Trust committee, foreseeing yet another spell in prison for Kees, voted and agreed to forward enough money to cover the amount demanded by the Dutch authorities. They also agreed to send some extra money each month for Julius ter Beek to spend discreetly on the family. On no account were the Boekes to find out about the continuing deception.

As William Cadbury had promised, he went out to visit Beatrice and her family in April, 1926. He was shocked by what he saw.

Het Boschhuis was in a run-down state. To him it was virtually derelict. The paintwork was in dire need of attention. The walls were grimy and the floors looked to have suffered from the constant flow of traffic through the house. People were forever coming and going in this 'open house'. Basic kitchen utensils were missing, either (William guessed) because they had not been replaced after the bailiffs had auctioned off these items, or because the vagrants who seemed to wander in and out of the house at will had stolen them.

The once-beautiful library that had housed many valuable first editions was ruined – by theft and from a recent police raid on the house, (carried out by constables looking to find evidence proving Kees was a spy).

More than the damage to the house, William was very worried about Beatrice. She was infuriatingly philosophical about their troubles and still stubbornly refusing financial help, insisting that everything was fine. Material possessions were unimportant, she said. So what if things had been taken from the house? It was only people trying to annoy them and deflect them from their true purpose. To add to William's frustration, he had been unable to persuade Beatrice to reconsider her decision to allow Kees to teach their girls himself, especially as the money was there to pay for their education.

William was at a loss as to what to do next. On his return, he suggested to Tom Hackett that the Boeke Trust increase their yearly visit to Bilthoven to twice a year. In the end, it was decided there would be one visit from the Trust and one from a member of the Cadbury family.

He must have been struck by the irony. Here he was, a director of Cadbury (a successful family firm with a growing reputation around the world) and a former Lord Mayor of Birmingham, with a sister living in poverty in a remote Dutch town. If ever the press got hold of the story they would have a field day. Never mind that it was Beatrice's choice to live that way.

It was at best an embarrassment, and at worst, utterly infuriating, and potentially life-threatening for the children.

After William's report, the Boeke Trust committee sent Tom Hackett and Kathleen Cox out to Bilthoven again in June, 1926.

They saw for themselves that the children were indeed being taught by Kees. They visited the girls in their little classroom on the Van der Helstlaan and, although the girls seemed happy enough, Tom and Kathleen were worried by the unconventional set-up. The issue was weighing particularly heavily on Kathleen, as she was in poor health and wanted to ensure the issue of the Boeke girls' education was resolved before she was forced to retire. During a quiet moment, when neither Beatrice nor Kees were present, Kathleen took the oldest girls, Helen and Emma, aside and said, "You must let me know if you want proper training for a career."

Before the visit, the Boeke Trust had authorised the sum of £100 to be spent on the Boeke family. To Beatrice this was an extravagance she thought quite unnecessary. The money was spent on repairs to and redecoration of the house, more clothes for the children, sets of household linen (to replace what had gone missing) and some general household items, such as a new set of crockery. Beatrice accepted these gifts very reluctantly because she knew the intentions of the Trust members were essentially kind. But she would only allow the most basic items to be bought, so the clothes were simple and the shoes made of rubber, but at least the children could be dressed semi-respectably.

The committee was also deeply concerned about the general health and well-being of the Boeke family. They made repeated enquiries through their Dutch contacts to try and find out who the family doctor was. Were they registered with a dentist? The trust members were frustrated they could not find out. Beatrice would never ask for help so it was a constant guessing game to anticipate what the family needed, even down to the right-sized shoes for the children.

*

Back at the Bournville Works, the Boeke Trust members were

facing difficult questions from the Cadbury workers. Many of them had never really understood the aims of the Trust. There was widespread puzzlement about what the money from Beatrice's legacy was supposed to be used for, and this confusion was felt even amongst the more educated and politically enlightened workers who might have been sympathetic to the Boekes' ideals (Tom Hackett's '5 to 10%' of workers interested in socialism). What had triggered their grumbles was the news that the Boeke Trust had funded the International Conference in Birmingham that Julius had attended. (This was in keeping with Beatrice and Kees's aims of promoting internationalism and peace.)

Tom received a letter from the spokesman for the Carpenters' Shop Committee, the union of carpenters employed at the Works. He opened it with a heavy heart, having already had an inkling of what was inside. It was a request for two questions to be put to the Boeke Trust: 'Do the Boeke Trust Committee consider the amount of money spent on international conferences justified by the results?' And the second: 'Will the Boeke Trust Committee ask the delegates on their return [from the conference] to give the workers a restatement of the ideas underlying the action of the Boeke family?' Clearly, the Carpenters' Shop Committee was not too impressed by how the income from Beatrice's legacy was being spent and wanted it to be put to more immediately beneficial use.

The Trust gave a robust response. They could hardly do otherwise. The conferences were arranged in the interest of international peace, they said, and yes, they were prepared to say the money spent was justified by the results. But it was difficult for the Trust members: they were, to an extent, stuck in the middle.

*

Beatrice was pleased that Kees had found a renewed zest for life through his project of teaching his daughters. He was coming out of his depression, and was buoyed by the fact that all over Europe and indeed the world, there was a rethink of children's education. Educationalists, philosophers and general commentators expressed the view that a widespread failure in the education system was responsible (in part) for war. A more progressive system would encourage international co-operation and remove the prejudices and barriers to lasting peace. A.S. Neill's Summerhill School was one of the original free-thinking schools of this kind.

During the 1920s, experimental schools were springing up all over the world, encouraged by a new movement founded in Britain by Beatrice Ensor, called the New Education Fellowship. It grew out of the idealism that followed the First World War. Kees embraced these new ideas.

The Boeke Trust was cheered by this news and relieved that the couple seemed to have settled down at last. There were no further arrests or imprisonments in 1926. *Het Boschhuis* had been redecorated. And the Trust had ensured a financial support system for the Boeke family was in place, albeit a surreptitious one, which did not sit easily with their consciences.

But then, in August 1926, an alarming piece of news reached the Boeke Trust committee. The minutes of the crisis meeting called to discuss the issue recorded it as follows:

> 'The committee were informed of the developments that had taken place [in Bilthoven] in the last few weeks. Several men, probably of the tramp type, had settled down in the 'Boschhuis' and vicinity and were helping themselves to food as well as interfering with the arrangements for the family ... Mr and Mrs Boeke had finally decided that they and their children could no longer continue to live in the Boschuuis. Mr and Mrs Boeke had further decided that ... the family would live in two tents on a piece of land belonging to their friends.'

*

On and off for the last few years, Beatrice and Kees had been plagued by burglars and people wandering in and out of their home. The news had spread on the grapevine that in Bilthoven there was a house where it was possible to get free board and lodging from a kind-hearted couple, who would ask for nothing in return.

Whilst it was irritating to have food, books or their other possessions stolen, Beatrice and Kees had been determined to stick with their open-door policy. To have put locks on the doors again would have been an admission of failure. They had learned to live with these annoyances, such was their passionate faith in the goodness of mankind. People were only driven to commit acts of theft when they were in desperate circumstances, they told themselves and each other.

But neither could deny the fact that lately there had been an escalation in the pilfering. To begin with, their 'guests' used to let themselves into *Het Boschhuis* to spend a night on the living room floor, before moving on the next day. Now it seemed that some vagrants were set on squatting there and occupying the entire ground floor permanently.

For a short time the family continued to live upstairs, but Beatrice and Kees could see no end to the invasion. It was hard to bear the suspicion that people were laughing behind their backs at this latest trouble. One of their detractors took great delight in mentioning that many of their books (including some of the valuable first editions) had been seen on sale in a second-hand bookshop in Utrecht.

What to do? They would have to get away for a while. As it was summer-time, Beatrice and Kees decided to take the children to the countryside nearby to take a break from the situation while they considered prayerfully what to do next.

They had left themselves with no practical alternative. Staying in the house could be dangerous for the children. Calling upon the police to evict the vagrants was equally unthinkable. After all, the couple had rejected the state and not paid tax for the last three years. It would have been grossly hypocritical of them to ask the law to help them, even if they had wanted to. In any case, they suspected that the police (who had already planted agents within their Community Council group) may have encouraged the squatters to move in, in an attempt to force them to capitulate with the authorities.

Kees heard from a friend that they could have the loan of several large tents if they wanted to go camping. (Ironically, these were ex-army tents, but he was not going to quibble over that.) What could be better than to take the family on a camping holiday to Den Dolder, just two miles away and near the Bilthoven-to-Zeist railway line? It was the summer holidays and time for the children to have some fun. Beatrice reassured the children it was nothing to worry about. On the contrary, it was going to be a great adventure.

Everyone was excited. Only five-year-old Daniel, who had been a sickly child, was to stay behind at *Het Boschhuis* in the care of one of the couple's friends, Stella Geisberts, who was living there at the time. Daniel could join them in the daytime but was not strong enough to 'rough it' by sleeping in a tent at night.

They found a spot in a wooded area full of pine trees and sandy hillocks. A large circular tent, which came with a wooden floor, would serve as the family's sleeping tent. A second tent, of similar size, would be the kitchen and dining tent. For a time, a couple of their friends from *Het Boschhuis* joined them. Kees erected some wooden 'walls' to section off the sleeping tent to give a modicum of privacy to the family. Beatrice was proud to see her husband using his carpentry skills once again.

A nearby water pipe supplied them with cold water. They dug a hole in the ground for their toiletry needs. The weather in August 1926 was kind. Day after day, dawn broke and the air was already warm and balmy, turning into brilliant midday sunshine that tanned the children's pale faces.

For Beatrice it was an intensely happy summer in which they lived almost entirely outdoors. The children slipped into a routine, spending their days roaming the woods or retreating to their own little 'room' in the tent to play with toys brought over from home. In the evening there would be long family walks into De Pan and when night-time fell, they would lie at the entrance to the tent, gazing up at the sky. Beatrice taught the children the names of the planets and stars. The camping and star-gazing recalled her own idyllic family holidays in Egypt with her parents.

She did not want to return but September and the new 'school' term was approaching.

The situation at *Het Boschhuis* had not improved during the family's absence. If anything, it was worse than ever. One day Stella turned up at the tents to say that a large family from Amsterdam, apparently homeless and destitute, had installed themselves in the house. They had helped themselves to food from the larder, including the two eggs that were for Daniel's breakfast. Beatrice and Kees discussed what to do. There was nothing for it but stay put in the tents, even if it meant abandoning *Het Boschhuis* entirely.

September beckoned and Daniel and Candia went back to the Montessori School, Candia returning each night to the tents. Theodora had turned three and was due to start at the nursery, too. So poor were the family finances that Theodora did not yet possess a pair of shoes of her own and so had to be taken by bicycle to school each day, sitting on the handlebars.

*

At the August meeting, during which the Boeke Trust had discussed the 'tent situation', the committee members agreed to do nothing for the time being, but to wait and monitor the state of affairs. But two months later, circumstances had reached crisis point.

October 1926 proved to be the rainiest month on record in Den Dolder. The tents developed leaks and one of the children was forced to sleep with an umbrella over her head, although this solution was no real protection against the heavy downfall. Beatrice tried to make light of the situation and would not consider asking for help from her family back home. She was prepared to stay in the tents all winter if need be.

But Barrow, who was still acting as the Cadbury Chairman, caught wind of what was going on in Holland. It is not known who raised the alarm but it was likely to have been one of Beatrice and Kees's concerned friends worried by the family's precarious situation.

By now Barrow had reached the limits of his patience. He and Geraldine had prayed earnestly for Beatrice and her family; he had tried to avoid being judgemental or condemnatory, but, really, there seemed to be no end to the troubles in Bilthoven. It was time he put his foot down and sorted out these absurd living arrangements.

Barrow took leave from the factory and together with Geraldine he launched a mission to rescue his six nieces and one nephew from their perilous state.

He and his wife caught the boat to Holland and then the train to Bilthoven. When they arrived at the Den Dolder camp, the family was in a sorry state. To humour his sister, whom he did not want to criticise overtly – knowing it would be counterproductive – Barrow and Geraldine spent a day with the family camping. Geraldine's careful eye looked out for signs of malnourishment in the children. Their dirty faces, forlorn and pinched with cold, were like poster girls (and boy) for Save the Children or some other charity for underprivileged children. When Candia climbed onto her lap, Geraldine discreetly checked her fingernails and underneath her eyes. She was probably anaemic.

Ironically, Barrow was a huge advocate of the health benefits of outdoor living. As a young man he had been impressed by the open-air schools he had seen in Germany, and in 1911 had converted Uffculme, their childhood home, into an open-air hospital and school. But if his goal had been to protect the poor children of Birmingham from the effects of malnutrition and poverty he surely had a duty to act with his own nieces and nephew. Beatrice sensed the controlled anger quietly seething inside her brother, and she did not offer any defence. Nor did she need to be cajoled into accepting help. That moment of realisation had come: it was time to give up the tents.

It was time for her and Kees to compromise.

*

Barrow's first action was to find the family an alternative place to live. Clearly, the situation at *Het Boschhuis* had become untenable and Barrow was not prepared to endanger the children by letting them return. He found a rented cottage for the family on Koekoeklaan (Cuckoo Lane) in a working-class quarter of Bilthoven. After the spaciousness of their previous home, it was a tiny dwelling. But while Barrow would have preferred his sister to be somewhere larger and in more salubrious surroundings, he guessed that anywhere too grand would be refused. The new house was near to the train station and around the corner from the post office. If Beatrice and Kees saw any irony in this (the railways and the postal service being part of their Break with the State boycott) they did not comment. At least they had a roof that did not leak. After two months of outdoor living, they were in no position to reject Barrow's generous offer.

The worker's cottage that Barrow chose was much less modest even than one of the typical workers' houses in Bournville that their Uncle George had built for their own factory workers. The new house was in fact similar in vision to the houses at Bournville, in that it was one of a row of workers' dwellings built by the Utrecht Building Association. When Kees realised that it was one

187

of the houses he had actually worked on during his brief period as a carpenter, it made the pill of failure a little less bitter to swallow. Barrow asked himself what their father, Richard Cadbury, would have made to see his youngest daughter living in such a humble dwelling.

Beatrice and Kees did not argue when Barrow told them that he had paid a year's rent on the house. It did not need to be said that he would continue to pay the rent. Barrow and Geraldine were not prepared to leave Bilthoven until they had helped Beatrice and Kees rescue their few remaining possessions from *Het Boschhuis* and moved them in to their new home. The couple had perhaps learned a salutary lesson, Barrow hoped, which meant they would never go to such extremes again.

*

Chastened and indeed disillusioned by the failure of their attempt to create a more peaceful and fairer society, Beatrice and Kees spent a quiet Christmas in the Cuckoo Lane house.

It measured twenty-five square feet, with two rooms downstairs, another storey upstairs, plus an attic room accessed via a steep staircase. Beatrice was relieved to see the house had a 'douche cell' (or shower room), which seemed like untold luxury after two months of living in tents and bathing in streams.

Downstairs, the front room led into a living room. At one end of the room was a stove with a tiny kitchen area. There was room for Kees's piano at the other end, but once the couple's (now battered) dining table was brought from *Het Boschhuis*, the room was all but filled. Space was at a premium. The front room would also have to serve as Beatrice and Kees's bedroom, along with their two youngest, Daniel and Theodora. The four of them would have to sleep together on the couch.

On the first floor there were two more rooms: a tiny bedroom which was given to Stella, who was moving in with them to help look after the children, and the shower room. The attic room would have to do for the older children: Helen, Emma, Paula, Julia and Candia. Each night Beatrice climbed the steep staircase to read the girls their favourite story (at least so she believed) of the 'Little Peppers'. This was a series of children's books about a mother and her five children who are living in poverty in their 'little brown house', who dream of rescue by a rich gentleman:

> "'Poor things!' she would say to herself, "they haven't had any bringing up; they've just scrambled up!" And then she would set her lips together tightly, and fly at her work faster than ever. "I must get schooling for them some way, but I don't see how!'"

The similarity between the lives of the Boeke children and the 'Little Peppers' must have been only too apparent. They had been reduced to charity cases.

*

As they settled into the house, Beatrice was determined to be cheerful in the face of adversity. On the positive side, the house was cosy and dry. Although in a more densely-populated area than *Het Boschhuis*, there were park areas nearby where the children could play.

Although Beatrice was young at heart, the years of stress had taken their toll. Photos from her early forties showed her looking even more gaunt and white-haired. Kees, on the other hand, some six months younger than his wife, had no signs of grey and his hairline was only slightly receding. In material terms the house was poorly suited to a middle-aged couple with seven children between the ages of fourteen and three. But at least they were settled, together and in a stable environment.

However, Kees still had no proper job that would provide a reliable income. What was the family going to live on? The Boeke Trust could not go on supporting the family indefinitely. The committee members themselves were beginning to tire of the subterfuge of sending over a small sum of money each month so that friends of the Boekes could keep them supplied with essentials – bread, eggs, milk, and cream. Kathleen Cox, who – along with Tom Hackett – had been Beatrice's greatest ally was now in poor health. At the end of 1926, she retired from the Bournville Works and stepped down from The Boeke Trust.

As far back as 1922, the article published in the *New York Times* had forewarned of the problems in store for Beatrice when she surrendered all claims on her Cadbury legacy. Its chilling assessment that she had impoverished herself seemed only too accurate.

But it was Kees's attempt to provide education for his children that would prove a vital lifeline in the final chapters in the life of Beatrice and her family.

Part IV
The School Years

10

The Werkplaats:
A New Kind of School,
1927-1937

THE THREE YEARS from 1927 to 1929 were happier ones; Beatrice welcomed this period of calm and relative tranquility after the stormy years triggered by the 'Break with the State' campaign. The fervent activism of the early 1920s had burnt itself out to be replaced with a quiet period where the family retreated into itself.

The children made friends easily with the locals, and spent many happy hours learning simple street games of marbles and skipping or spinning tops. Free-spirited Daniel, now aged six, loved to escape with his neighbourhood friends from morning until dusk only to come back 'as black as a sheep'.

The Boeke girls noticed an immediate change in their parents. Instead of the constant meetings in the evenings, the family would sit around the table for supper, and afterwards their father would read aloud his favourite extracts from Shakespeare, or play a few bars from Bach on the piano. The family bonds were renewed and strengthened once more.

Kees resumed the work of teaching his children and a few of their friends at the little room in Mrs Kerdijk's house. Beatrice was relieved he had this activity to occupy him. Mrs van Kooten, one of her neighbours, became a good friend to Beatrice. She began to look forward to a time of rest and consolidation.

But if 1926 was marked by the 'episode of the tents' then 1927 would be characterised by a string of alarming family illnesses. The children had been under considerable physical and emotional stress during recent years; and it was highly probable that the period of outdoor living had weakened their immune systems.

The first to become ill was Theodora. She was a sweet-natured, lovable child, who had just turned four in the spring of 1927. One morning she woke up complaining of earache. When bloody pus began to leak out of her ear, Beatrice knew she must have a serious ear infection that required medical treatment. Soon she was howling, clearly in agony, and she was rushed to the Diaconessenhuis, a hospital in Leiden, about thirty miles away.

Theodora was so distressed at the thought of being parted from her mother that the doctors made an exception to their normal regulations and allowed Beatrice to sleep in her hospital room. By now Beatrice had begun to experience the tell-tale signs of pregnancy once again. It had been four years since the birth of Theodora and now, at the age of forty-three, Beatrice was a little surprised to have conceived again.

A month or so later, Daniel contracted measles and was admitted to the same hospital. The fees were later taken care of by Barrow and Geraldine. Now Beatrice was pregnant it was too risky for her to visit Daniel. Instead, Stella spent many hours at his bedside while Beatrice could only stand and watch her son through the window.

During the hours of anxiety at the hospital, Beatrice had time for reflection. Uncomfortable thoughts began to emerge about the stance that she and her husband had taken, and the way they had been living. Although she and Kees had supported each other without question, she could not ignore the material hardships the children had suffered. Had it been justified, or had they been almost arrogant in believing their way of living – their life of service to Christ – was right? She tried to quell these troubling thoughts as she kept her vigil outside her ailing son's room.

Both children recovered, thankfully, and in December Beatrice felt the onset of early labour pains. Her next child was due. She intended to give birth at home in Koekoelaan with her neighbour, Mrs van Kooten, assisting. Healthcare did not come cheaply and there was no money for expensive maternity care fees. But Geraldine, Barrow's wife, came over to Holland again and firmly insisted she go back – at Geraldine's expense – to the Diaconessenhuis to have the baby. Whereas Beatrice would once have stubbornly refused this offer of help, she now acquiesced.

It was a decision that probably saved her life.

She checked into the hospital and on 10th December, 1927, she safely delivered the eighth and last of their children. It was another girl (their seventh) whom they named Marian, soon shortened to Maya.

But two days after the delivery, Beatrice began to show a worrying range of symptoms. Her cheeks became swollen and her eyes so puffy that she could barely see. She felt a crushing fatigue in her limbs so acute that she could not get out of bed.

Initially, the nurses thought it was just a reaction to the strain of giving birth but they soon realised that it was not simply post-natal tiredness. Something was seriously wrong. At his wife's bedside, Kees was immediately transported back to that time in Brummana when Beatrice fell ill immediately following the birth of their first child, Helen.

The doctor, an eminent physician called Dr. Steyns, diagnosed the problem as an auto-immune form of nephritis, or an inflammation of the kidneys, which was potentially life-threatening. Her treatment lasted five weeks and consisted of a range of self-vaccine injections. Had Beatrice stuck with her original plan of giving birth at home she may well have lost her life. Yet again she had reason to be grateful to the care and intervention – both financial and practical – of the Cadbury family. She had wanted to escape the privilege she had been born into and yet it seemed she could not.

The slow weeks of recovery brought yet more time for taking stock of her situation.

When Beatrice was well enough, she returned home to a joyous welcome from her much-relieved family, and life carried on. Kees devoted most of 1928 to teaching his children. He was not an educationalist, but he had an instinct for applying a scientific approach to learning. And it seemed to be paying off. The home school had grown to seventeen pupils. Seven of these were the Boeke children, but the other ten came from the children of friends who were sympathetic to Kees's ideals and willing to take a chance on putting their children's minds into Kees's hands.

So the family was settled and the home school seemingly well-established. But at the beginning of the autumn term in 1928, after only a year and a half, Kees was in trouble again with the authorities, in spite of the fact that he had retreated entirely from public life, preferring instead to be left alone.

One evening in September, Kees came home from the school in a furious mood. Over supper he told Beatrice that a school inspector had turned up at Mrs Kerdijk's house out of the blue and had asked to see inside the premises. Kees duly obliged, showing him the light-filled 'classroom' with the heads of his children and their friends bowed in concentration. He was proud of the individual lessons he had planned for each of the pupils and was very open with the unexpected visitor.

"And who is your head teacher?" the inspector asked.

"I am," Kees replied.

"But you aren't qualified," came the inarguable reply.

The inspector left with an ominous instruction that Kees must find a teacher who had been trained at primary school level to oversee the school. This was required under Dutch law. Should Kees fail to do this, he would face prosecution and possible imprisonment.

This presented a dilemma for the couple and they discussed possible solutions. What about your teaching certificate from England, Beatrice reminded him. However, although Kees had undergone some teacher training at the University of Birmingham, the certificate would not be recognised in Holland. What to do?

*

Since Beatrice and Kees had not formally rescinded their 'Break with the State' manifesto, Kees was not inclined to co-operate with the law. He had got into the habit of ignoring rulings of this kind, so he chose to do nothing, perhaps hoping the problem would go away or that the education authority would show leniency.

He was not that lucky.

Beatrice felt a sense of déjà vu when the court summons was posted through their letterbox, and their 'good friend', the policeman, Berkhoff, arrived to arrest Kees. Just as the school inspector had warned, Kees was prosecuted for failing to send his children to school and imprisoned for three weeks.

While he was in prison, however, an unexpected break occurred. A part-time French teacher who had been helping out at the home school, Mrs Wolswijk, had once been a head teacher herself. Without the prior knowledge of either Kees or Beatrice, she went to the education authority to say that in fact *she* was the head teacher of the school, and not Kees Boeke. Mrs Wolswijk's qualifications were scrutinised and deemed appropriate. Kees was subsequently released early from prison, without having had to betray his principles. Beatrice and the children were delighted to have daddy back home again.

At this point their luck improved further when a family friend, Mrs Willie Bosman, made a donation to enable the construction of purpose-built school premises. The Boeke Trust committee, hearing of this new development, were keen to offer financial support, too, and agreed that a family home for the Boeke family should be funded and built next door to the new school. Beatrice and Kees found an ideal location on a leafy street called Hobbemalaan, a couple of minutes from the home school.

In the middle of all the building work, Beatrice's sister, Helen, came to Bilthoven to visit. The children were delighted to see their auntie. Beatrice, too, was overjoyed since having given up the use of a passport she was dependent on family visits to Holland.

Helen Alexander had had a few difficult years since the death of her husband, Charles, in October 1920. To her astonishment, she had received a proposal of marriage from an American suitor – a widower named Dr Amzi Clarence Dixon – who was part of the evangelical circuit she and Charles had shared. Helen and Amzi had married in 1924 but a year and a half later he had died of spinal cancer. Helen, after her brief second chance of happiness, was now resigned to widowhood and threw her energies into charitable work, and being a good auntie to her many nieces and nephews, who visited her at Tennessee.

The two sisters were able to renew the sibling bond, walking arm-in-arm from Koekoelaan to Hobbemalaan to see the construction of the new school taking shape. Privately, Helen was shocked at how tiny her sister's house was and her humble way of living. She also thought the building work on the new house and school was taking an awfully long time but she was careful not to criticise or take the enjoyment away from Beatrice's excitement.

The new two-storey house built at Hobbemalaan 76 was so much more spacious; compared to their previous home it felt positively palatial. Beatrice marvelled as the new bathroom and shower were installed. The children danced around at the prospect of having their own rooms. At last everyone could have privacy again; including Beatrice and Kees, who would no longer have to share with Daniel, Theodora and baby Marian.

The new school building was also an untold improvement on the home school. It had a central teaching room, with a number of smaller rooms that fanned it in a semi-circle. The building faced south and had large windows to maximise the warmth from the sun.

Everyone lent a hand on moving day, including the children and their friends. Together, they ferried all their possessions on carts, wheelbarrows and bikes. Even a big wooden barn was dismantled and carried to Hobbemalaan with much hilarity. Beatrice would later recall how the event lived on in the annals of the school, as 'the walking barn with its sixteen pairs of feet'.

The Werkplaats school, as it came to be known, officially opened in July, 1929. The one thing it lacked was a central heating system. Dutch winters were fierce, and that winter lessons could not start until the children had gone through a range of outdoor gymnastics and stretching exercises designed to get their circulation going. This was followed by a shower and vigorous rubbing down – all preparation to ward off the icy chill of the classroom.

On hearing of this, the Boeke Trust committee agreed to contribute £100 so that proper heating could be installed in the building.

The excitement of the school opening was tempered by anxiety over more illness within the Boeke family. Daniel, now eight, was diagnosed with appendicitis and ten-year-old Candia needed surgery to her ear following a serious infection. Both children were operated on in the same day.

These illnesses focused Beatrice's mind once again on the children and the responsibilities that she and Kees, as parents, had towards them. Their 'Break with the State' doctrine had forced them into a rigid and uncompromising position but now, not for the first time, a doubt crept into both her and Kees's hearts about the difficulties they had put their children through. There was a gradual softening in their approach and, to the surprise of the Boeke Trust committee, Beatrice and Kees were finally ready to allow the Trust to support the further education of the older children.

Helen was now seventeen and had gone through three years of being taught by daddy. She was desperate to explore new horizons. With her parents' blessing, and the financial support of the Boeke Trust, Helen went to Rotterdam to study for a teaching certificate, although it is not known whether the initial idea of training to be a teacher was hers or her parents. She stayed with a family friend, Lily Boon, while she studied and she passed the exam on her second attempt. She then returned to teach at the Werkplaats. Emma followed the same route a year later.

By this time Beatrice was giving serious thought to her attitude towards the use of money. Kees was also realising the sheer impracticality of running the school without being able to handle the money paid in fees himself. (At first, parental contributions to the school were entirely voluntary but when a fee was introduced, it was done so on a sliding scale depending on the financial circumstances of the parents.) For the time being at the school, they got around the problem by appointing their next-door neighbour, Bettie Kerdijk, in the role of a school administrator responsible for collecting school fees. But their position was starting to look ridiculous even to them.

*

Through his lessons Kees began to formulate an educational ethos that took a child's needs and their motivation to learn as the starting point. The name he decided to give the school was De Werkplaats Kindergemeenschap (Children's Community Workshop), which became known simply as The Werkplaats.

In typical Kees fashion, he challenged the usual educational terminology, preferring instead to create his own ideology. At the school, the pupils were named 'Workers' while the teachers were classified as the 'Helpers' (later 'Fellow Workers'). The new premises had been built with a view to accommodating up to fifty children. When term officially began that September, twenty 'Workers' had been registered by their parents. Numbers grew slowly but consistently year by year. The costs were kept down as far as possible and many of the school's early 'Helpers' worked without receiving a salary at all.

Kees said of the name, The Werkplaats (The Workplace or Workshop):

'The reason why I chose this name is that I always associate school with being instructed, with being taught. It was not my intention to teach these children, rather to enable them to develop their own skills, according to their personal aptitude … what I wanted to try and create was in fact a place to work, hence the name Workplace.'

Beatrice's contribution to the school was important. Although it was very much Kees's project to begin with, she shaped the school hugely in her own quiet way. Despite her hands being full with her own children, she was persuaded to take over some of the teaching of English, although she had concerns initially about being up to the job. "I'm afraid I have no certificate or degree," she said to the other Helpers. But that did not matter. Her warm and motherly manner made her an instant hit with the pupils, or 'Workers'. For the children, cleaning and tidying the school, and performing other duties, was a pleasure when it earned them a smile from dear 'Betty'.

One of Beatrice's friends wrote:

'From Betty came warmth and understanding, and a mind that could never think meanly of anyone or dwell on the unpleasant side of her fellow creatures, but behaved like a good mother who loves all those in her care. She was a person you felt to whom you could go with all your troubles and worries.'

She and Kees discussed ideas about the school, usually on a daily basis. He was slowly finding his way out of the political wilderness and had begun to write articles for the magazine 'Vernieuwing' (literally, 'Renewal'), which was an important vehicle for talking about modernisation. The Werkplaats became part of the Dutch branch of the New Education Fellowship (NEF).

One of the important principles of The Werkplaats was that of foreign language education. Kees and Beatrice wanted all the children at the school to be multi-lingual, being convinced that the study of other languages, and their cultures, was the only way to break down racial barriers and build harmonious international relations.

*

In the early 1930s the school continued to run on a shoestring. The high staff turnover was a continual headache. Many good teachers would have liked to stay but as soon as they started families of their own they were often compelled to leave in search of a higher salary. Mrs Kerdijk's daughter was roped in to help, along with Helen and Emma, who were newly-qualified teachers. However, word of the school was starting to spread across Holland and beyond, and its methods inspired some to action. A married couple, Joop and Willie Westerweel, heard about the school and volunteered their services as teachers in return for sharing the Boeke household for a time. Two trained teachers from Germany, Heinrich and Ilsa von der Dunk, also offered to work at the school for next to nothing. The school had no problem attracting teachers, no doubt because of Kees's exciting educational vision, but retaining the staff on little or no salary was difficult. Stella Geisberts became the school secretary, as she was not needed to help so much with the Boeke children at home, now they were all growing up.

The Werkplaats was truly progressive and as the years went on Kees began to formulate a set of principles to underpin the discussions about what the purpose of education should be. He became something of the evangelist again, but the fervent activism of the 1920s was replaced with a more mellowed outlook. No longer did he see the world in apocalyptic terms.

He began recording all his ideas about the philosophy behind The Werkplaats in one place. (His notes were eventually published in book form in 1934, as De Werkplaats Kindergemeenschap – or 'Children's Community Workshop'.) To educational experts and commentators, the ethos at The Werkplaats appeared to turn conventional wisdom completely on its head.

There were no marks or grades given to school work, in order to eradicate the competitive element which, Kees believed, discouraged less able children whilst encouraging faster children to become 'conceited', or even 'reckless'. Every Worker at the school should have his or her work recognised and valued.

The aim was to build a micro-community, where the children as well as the adults took responsibility for working together co-operatively. The fact The Werkplaats had such a limited budget meant that the 'Workers' took on some of the care-taking jobs normally done by adults. For example, growing vegetables in the school garden, then cooking them and eating together taught the children about the value of food. The children were also expected to clean their classroom each morning (there being no money for cleaners) and undertake minor repairs. Very quickly there was a strong sense of ownership and pride in the school. It was not just boring chores, however. Music, exercise and dance were considered a key part of the educational experience. Kees wrote many of his own songs, which the children learned by heart.

There was no prescribed curriculum. Children worked at their own pace on individualised learning programmes, much as the Boeke children had done when Kees had first started home-schooling them in 1926. This did not mean a chaotic system, however. Kees had a love of order as well as of freedom. The school was always clean and tidy and he implemented a set of learning cards for each Worker that described the standard that needed to be reached. This form of record-keeping evolved into what became known as the Werkplaats Test System.

The Werkplaats welcomed children of all ages and did not separate the children into 'artificial' stages, such as primary or secondary, or by year group.

Kees believed that children had a natural instinct for play, which should be nurtured with outdoor activity and plenty of free and 'unregulated' time. The role of the teacher (Helper) was to nurture the 'Workers', making sure the tools and equipment they needed were within easy reach. This approach borrowed heavily from the Montessori method of teaching.

Experiences outside the classroom were just as valuable as those in school. School trips were a regular feature of life at The Werkplaats, but even then the trips bore the Boeke stamp of unconventionality. The tradition of the Night Walk was established soon after the school opened. The children were told to put on their pyjamas and dressing gowns and to assemble near the woods at eleven o'clock. From their meeting point, Kees and Beatrice led the children through the woods to experience the wonders of nature in the stillness of the night. For children bred in the town, it was an opportunity to experience nature directly. Being in the dark concentrated the other senses so the sounds of birds, the smell of night flowers, the feel of branches against their legs offered a form of experiential learning. The children listened in awe to the dawn chorus before trooping back home giddy with tiredness and the thrill of having stayed up all night. Experiencing the environment directly was a far more powerful form of learning than studying botany or wildlife from a textbook. Beatrice remembered this only too well from those holidays with her father, Richard, who had also led them to great adventures.

Another key principle of The Werkplaats was that there

would be no rewards or incentives (something Kees saw as equivalent to bribery) and, equally, no use or threat of physical punishment. Problems were discussed and resolved at a weekly General Meeting, called the Talkover, where the Workers and Helpers reached a consensus on what action, if any, needed to be taken. An important distinction began to be made in Kees's mind. Democracy was about the majority view holding sway but he believed it was futile to vote on action to be taken, rather than reaching agreement by consensus. A resolution could not be passed until it was acceptable to everyone. This principle of governance would later be termed Sociocracy.

It was not so very different from the Quaker way of resolving issues.

Although Beatrice and Kees were tied-up with the running of the school, they had not lost their commitment to social justice and the need to help those less fortunate. In some quarters of Bilthoven, slum areas had grown, in which housing conditions were cramped, with large families often living and sleeping in one room. Beatrice and Kees became troubled by the paucity of activities for older children: they seemed to have nowhere to go and nothing to do once their younger siblings had fallen asleep. Kees and two of the other Werkplaats teachers decided to put on evening classes in woodwork and practical crafts. Undoubtedly, Kees was influenced by Beatrice and her memories of Richard Cadbury's tireless work with his Adult School classes.

By 1932, it had been ten years since Beatrice had given away her fortune and nine years since they had lived their lives without handling money. Their attitudes had undoubtedly become more moderate in recent times but Beatrice and Kees were about to make a surprising discovery that brought them up sharp.

As Beatrice had already suspected, they finally discovered that the food left for them by their friends had been bought with money that had come directly from the Boeke Trust. True, Beatrice had, in the most extreme circumstances, been willing to accept help from her brothers, Barrow and William. She had even agreed, albeit reluctantly, to accept the gifts of clothing for the children from the Boeke Trust and, more recently, money towards the girls' further education. But to realise that the Boeke Trust had acted behind their backs was a profound shock. Yet she also acknowledged to herself that its members had been acting out of almost parental interest and with genuine care and concern.

At first, Kees pleaded with the trustees not to continue their financial help but Beatrice and Kees realised that they had an opportunity to help secure the future of the school. They asked if the money could go to The Werkplaats and, from 1932 onwards, the Trust gave the school a regular sum that was divided amongst all the teachers to subsidise their low wages. Beatrice and Kees's consciences were salved because the money was being used for educational purposes. The Trust was happy because if the school could be secured then this would have a positive impact on the stability of the Boeke family.

Having compromised on this issue, Kees felt it was now time to begin using money again, which he did on 9th April 1935. Beatrice soon followed her husband.

This caused some agonising on her part, not least as to how the children would react. Beatrice felt it would be a 'painful disappointment' for the children to see their parents give up their stance; she feared her offspring would see this decision in terms of a 'treachery' against her and her husband's high ideals. The younger children born in Bilthoven had known no life other than their hand-to-mouth existence, where mummy and daddy had not used this strange thing called money. Other people paid to cross the toll road with coins; mummy offered eggs instead. Money was something to be shunned, even to be fearful of. Money made people evil – that was the message Beatrice and Kees had given their children. For Beatrice the idea of reversing this position was emotionally difficult.

And yet Beatrice occasionally had flashes of guilt. Their

attempt to live outside society had been a failure. It would be a gross delusion on their part to think otherwise. They had wanted to humble themselves before God, to prove that He would provide their daily bread. All they had actually done was to cause hardship for the children and put the responsibility for their welfare onto the shoulders of other people – their Dutch friends, the Cadbury relatives and of course the Boeke Trust. However noble it had been to live up to their ideals, the harsh truth was they had only survived with the constant interventions of Barrow and Geraldine, William, Helen, and Tom and Kathleen from the Boeke Trust.

As for their children, Beatrice's inner voice told her that she could no longer ignore the difficulties she and Kees had put them under. The conflicts with the authorities, the dependence on charity, the periods in prison, the illnesses: this was not the stuff of childhood. Children should be carefree and happy.

Although Beatrice had been acting out of 'Christ's command' in everything, she had also felt the implied criticism from her siblings (although neither Barrow, William nor Helen ever voiced their feelings outright). Still, she could see the concern in their eyes whenever they came to visit. She later reflected on this period:

'Many people blamed us and felt we were carrying things too far ... that we were acting in a way which was completely irresponsible towards the children. I can only say that our children were never out of our thoughts. We realised, at least to a certain extent, the difficulties which they experienced as a result of our actions.'

Beatrice had felt the same mixed feelings about the involvement of the Boeke Trust committee in her family's affairs. Every time the representatives, Tom and Kathleen, visited Bilthoven Beatrice had seen their none-too-discreet probing, checking for signs of illness or malnutrition in the children, trying to guess their shoe and clothes sizes, enquiring about whether the family was registered with a doctor and a dentist. The reality was that the yearly visits had been a strain for all of them.

It had not been a mistake to try to change society but by the mid-1930s Beatrice and Kees's doubts were crystallising. Perhaps it was not possible for *any* human being to remain entirely true to their beliefs. They had tried to live 'a life of Christ', to honour the teachings of the bible, to be 'perfect' in their beliefs and actions. And yet. Human beings were made with limitations and flaws. What if it had, in fact, been a form of sinful arrogance for her and Kees to believe that they could follow Christ's command, to believe that a human being could be 'perfect' in the same way the 'heavenly father' is perfect? It was disconcerting to feel this way.

In Bilthoven, Beatrice reflected, they had conducted their lives with an almost childlike simplicity. The application of their beliefs – their refusal to accept the law of the state before the law of God – had come at a price. It was now time to take stock, accept responsibility and think of the future.

Beatrice added up all the donations and gifts and medical care that had come out of her Cadbury legacy. It was only a small percentage of the total dividends derived yearly from her shares, and the bulk of her inheritance had, via the Boeke Trust, gone to charities, the funding of international conferences and helping the Cadbury workers through various schemes, such as holiday clubs, dental schemes and hardship funds. She knew that none of these should be discounted. Even so, she had failed in her attempt to change the fundamental nature of capitalism, as her original intention had been. Support for their own bold experiment, the 'Break with the State', had dwindled to nothing. Few people had followed their example and while they had had some admirers, they had far greater numbers of detractors.

Still, Beatrice was worried about the children's reaction to the decision to use money again and was fearful that it would harm them. She later wrote of her feelings:

'... to be unfaithful to what we believed to be our duty would only harm those dearest to us in their spiritual growth, although being faithful to our beliefs might bring material hardship and difficulties.'

The older children's emotions were mixed: a sadness perhaps yet also a huge relief. The younger children had never handled money and were only used to seeing their parents barter. They had been insulated from any notion of consumerism. Not for them the thrill of saving pocket money and seeing their bank balance mount up (as Beatrice had done as a child, encouraged by prudent Barrow). Never having participated in money systems, the younger Boeke children were financially illiterate and took longer to understand this new change in their lives.

*

In 1935, the couple planned a conference in Bilthoven again – this time with the Dutch branch of the New Education Fellowship (NEF). The group was interested in learning from other education systems around the world and Kees was voted chair of the group.

Having renounced their decision to stop using money, Beatrice and Kees looked at other areas of their state boycott and decided that they would apply for passports again. Beatrice was dying to return to England again to see her relatives in Birmingham and to take the children to see their many Cadbury cousins. Kees, for his part, no longer wanted to be constrained from international travel and communication. His Deportation Order of 1918, which had included a ban on him entering Britain again, was rescinded during Ramsay MacDonald's second period in office as Labour Prime Minister in the 1930s. (No doubt it helped that Ramsay MacDonald had been a friend of Beatrice's father, Richard, having been a visitor to their holiday home at Wynds Point, decades before.)

Kees went to England three times in 1935 to take part in the NEF conference in London and with Beatrice later on to visit Paula, now at St Andrew's University in Scotland, where she was studying music.

Beatrice thought Kees was back to his old self; his personal magnetism and ability to engage people was as strong as ever. As she watched him address the conference audience, it was reminiscent of their early days together in Birmingham and Bilthoven, during their anti-war protests, and those years of intoxicating idealism.

The following year brought more international activity for Kees. He was scheduled to appear at the NEF conference in Cheltenham (England) in the summer, as one of over twenty speakers from around the world talking about different aspects of education. He was back in his element again. He was desperately keen to promote what he was now beginning to call The Werkplaats Method. Many of the conference delegates attended his sessions on The Werkplaats and progressive schooling during the five-day conference course.

The support and enthusiasm he experienced during the trip encouraged him to formulate a plan. He was going to take on the Dutch education system, which he and many others believed was in desperate need of reform.

He networked at the conference with a view to creating an international centre for progressive schools, based in Bilthoven. Kees returned home and then right away left with Beatrice for Copenhagen for a meeting organised by the Boeke Trust some time between late August and early September.

However, by the time they returned to Bilthoven for the start of the new term on 7th September, 1936, Beatrice had become worried about Kees. He was coming up to his fifty-second birthday and in recent days had seemed exhausted and lacking his usual energies and enthusiasm. She recognised the signs of mental stress he had experienced after the International Fellowship of

Reconciliation conference in 1919. His mood was flat. He seemed depressed and would not be cheered up.

They were home in time for the start of the new Werkplaats term but Kees was clearly in need of a holiday. They managed another short trip to England, where Beatrice was glad to see her husband relaxing and where Kees's problem was diagnosed as a decaying tooth that had become infected. He was treated effectively although it took him some time to recover and during this recuperation they received news from Stella at The Werkplaats. The new year's intake, now around thirty pupils, had settled in badly. Beatrice and her husband rushed back home immediately to sort out the problem.

*

By 1936 the school had grown and now had a hundred children, with nine full-time and eighteen part-time teachers. The school had the capacity to grow in number, but the problem was how to manage the expansion without diluting the aims of the school. When The Werkplaats had opened in 1929, it had been designed for fifty children, which at the time had been the optimum number. They would now have to plan for growth.

The solution, which would allow the school to expand, whilst still keeping to this magic number, was to build a set of different school units, each based around a different foreign language.

More than ever, Beatrice and Kees believed that international co-operation and long-lasting peace could only be achieved if foreign language learning was built into the foundations of the school curriculum. They decided to build separate school units, where each unit would have its own medium of instruction. In the English unit, all subjects would be studied in English. There would also be French and German units that operated in the same way. The Dutch-speaking Helpers were teachers who tended to be fluent in these languages anyway and would have no problem teaching their subject specialism whatever the instructional language. Each child would spend a year in each unit, where both the language and the culture could be studied in detail.

Now fully recovered, Kees worked harder than ever. Beatrice had given up trying to persuade him to slow down, recognising that there was no stopping him during his 'up' times. He began to rise earlier and earlier, so that on one occasion (as Beatrice liked to tell it) she turned in late at one-thirty in the morning and met her husband on the stairs getting up for the day. "Good night, my darling," Beatrice said. "Good morning, my darling," Kees replied.

Kees had also turned his attention to teacher training. He believed that the root cause of the educational problems in Holland was the lack of adequate initial teacher training. He pioneered a course at The Werkplaats (called the Bilthoven Auxiliary Course), which provided compulsory training for any Helper employed at The Werkplaats. Representatives from the nearby Montessori School gave support, as many of the ideas and principles overlapped.

By the end of 1937, The Werkplaats was thriving and on its most stable footing yet. But a danger lurked that would threaten the very existence of the school, as well as the lives of the Boeke family and all their friends. The ideals of peace, love and international harmony that underpinned The Werkplaats' ethos were about to be blown apart.

11

Forces of War and the Final Surrender, 1938-1951

BEATRICE AND KEES had been following the slow but inexorable rise of Adolf Hitler and Nazism in Germany, and were outraged by the treatment of Jews in that country, many of whom had fled to Holland when the pogroms began in November, 1938. News of the *Kristallnacht*, or Night of the Broken Glass, when Jewish homes, synagogues and businesses in Germany were systematically ransacked and destroyed, sent shockwaves around the world. 30,000 Jews were rounded up and sent to concentration camps. Some of those Jews sought refuge in Holland but by the end of 1938 the numbers wanting to enter were so high that the Dutch government deemed it necessary to close its borders. To Beatrice, this action was almost as inhumane as the atrocities being carried out in Germany. Kees's response was to compose a song, 'Open Your Frontiers', to vent some of his anger towards the Dutch government at this shameful blindness to the humanitarian crisis.

But there would be no return to the activist days of the 1910s and 1920s, with their unremitting clashes of ideology. Beatrice and Kees were approaching their mid-fifties and they lacked the energy to lead and sustain a campaign of street protests and public meetings. Furthermore, they were no longer willing to risk imprisonment, or to compromise the safety of the children.

All their campaigning energies were now directed towards the field of educational reform. They still believed very passionately in peace, but they knew they had been unsuccessful in trying to change society by appealing to the Christian message of the inhumanity of war, or indeed the Marxist ideology of change through revolution. Their experiences told them that humankind had too much self-interest. The answer *had* to be in education and in creating small communities, where children learned from an early age the lessons of love, fellowship and respect for others.

Against the alarming situation in Europe, The Werkplaats should continue as normal, providing 'an oasis in a desert of confusion, despair and misery', as Beatrice put it. The priority had to be to keep things as normal as possible for the children. This was not to turn a blind eye to the plight faced by others, but rather to offer practical help where action could be taken.

One day one of the Workers at The Werkplaats, a boy called Philip, discovered a group of Jewish refugees from Poland living in the Den Dolder region. He was sorry for the children; they were bored and had nothing to do. Some had been separated from their parents and all were deeply traumatised. He wanted to help. Could they not attend lessons at The Werkplaats, he asked. The adults and children of the school rallied round. There was a large three-storey building, named *Eikenrode*, on the main road in Bilthoven that had fallen into disrepair, which would be an ideal location for another school. After a fund-raising initiative and the collection of donations from Bilthoven residents, the building was cleaned and kitted out for use as a school for the displaced Jewish children. It would be overseen by Mirjam Waterman (later Pinkhof), a teacher from Holland, who was Jewish, and employed at The Werkplaats. Candia Boeke, now aged nineteen, agreed to work there, too. Here was an excellent example of The Werkplaats philosophy in action, where the initiative had come first from the school children, who were helped by the adults where needed.

But amid the worrying time of tension and apprehension, there were some joyful events to look forward to. In the summer of 1939, the whole Boeke family went to Sanaan in Switzerland for a holiday, staying in a chalet belonging to Elizabeth Rotten, an old Quaker friend, who was famous for her peace and humanitarian work. Julia, who had been studying in England, was able to join the holiday party later. It was an idyllic family holiday, marred only by the worry that the British and French governments might declare war on Germany if the threatened invasion of Poland went ahead.

A holiday snap from the period showed the entire Boeke family, plus Paula's and Helen's fiancés, Paul Koning and Henrik (Henk) Jacobse, to whom the girls had recently become engaged to be married. Now they all looked handsome and well-dressed, in sharp contrast to the photographs from the 1920s where there had been visible signs of poverty. The two youngest girls, flaxen-haired Theodora and little Maya, wore their hair in plaits. The older girls, now grown women, looked smart in their puff-sleeved blouses and dresses with nipped-in waists, and their hair styled off their foreheads and sandals with slight heels. It was a world away from the shapeless, crumpled hand-me-down clothes and rubber shoes of their childhood.

Meanwhile, a visit from the Boeke Trust was scheduled for early September. Although Kathleen Cox had long since retired from the Bournville Works, the redoubtable Tom Hackett and his wife travelled again to Bilthoven, where a conference was being held. But on 3rd September, two days after the Nazis had invaded Poland, the devastating announcement came over the radio. Britain and France were now at war with Germany. Tom and Mrs Hackett had to rush back to England at once before they were trapped in Holland.

Britain's intervention in the war in 1939 affected Beatrice and Kees and The Werkplaats almost immediately, although Holland would not be directly involved in the conflict until the following May.

With border restrictions imposed by the war, it made it practically impossible for the Boeke Trust in Birmingham to be able to transfer money abroad. The regular income that The Werkplaats had come to rely on was now in jeopardy. Fearing this could mean the end of the school, Kees worked hard to secure extra funding in order to supplement the modest fees paid by parents. In the end, a local factory owner generously donated a large sum of money that meant a degree of financial security for The Werkplaats for the next few years.

Their own children continued to spread their wings. Paula and Paul Koning married in August, 1939, and three months later, on the day before her twenty-seventh birthday, Helen married Henk Jacobse. This was swiftly followed by another marriage. Emma, the second born, tied the knot with Herbertus (Bart) van der Wilt. The three eldest children were now settled and respectably married and soon the fourth eldest, Julia, would graduate with her International Teachers' Diploma. Her original ambition had been to become a doctor, but the school would need her.

*

The Dutch government, so it seemed, had wanted to remain neutral for as long as possible, resisting the many calls to join France and Britain in fighting the Nazi threat. But on 10th May, 1940, news came of Holland's invasion by German forces. A few days later, the Dutch Royal Family, including Queen Wilhelmina, Princess Juliana and her daughters, Beatrix and Irene, fled Holland to safety in Britain, escorted by a unit of Welsh and Irish Guards. For Beatrice and her family, however, there would be no escape. Waking one morning to the roar of overhead planes and gunfire,

Beatrice was filled with dread. The flashing red and orange sky told her that the Germans were moving in. Rotterdam fell first, then Utrecht. Bilthoven would surely be next.

Up to now, The Werkplaats had functioned as a micro-community of its own. The people who taught there did so out of moral conviction first – the salary was a secondary consideration. Joop Westerweel (who together with his wife, Willie, had volunteered their services when the school began) had been appointed as school principal. Now the Westerweels, along with Mirjam Waterman, were called to become part of the underground Dutch resistance movement, helping Jews to escape from persecution.

The Werkplaats stood out as a beacon of security and peace; Beatrice and Kees knew that their beliefs in international co-operation and peace could not be more anathema to the German occupiers. So their focus remained on trying to shield the schoolchildren from the emotional stress and anxiety caused by the war. Kees, in particular, was desperate that the school should not be forced to close. It was his life's work. But trouble did not materialise – at least not at first. The Germans appeared to be conciliatory and, to begin with, life carried on much as it had done before the Occupation.

The Werkplaats had an extensive musical programme up to and during the war years. Music and song kept the spirit alive; it nurtured the soul, gave solace and also strength to remain resolute in the face of intimidation (although there were never any overt anti-Nazism protests involving the schoolchildren). Kees was not only a gifted pianist, violinist and composer himself, but he also believed music could be played and sung by anyone, regardless of their level of talent; he had the knack of encouraging everyone to give their best performance. The school plays and concerts at The Werkplaats were highly participative affairs. Productions of Shakespeare, including 'Hamlet', were put on during the war years, and there was a spectacular production of Bach's *St Matthew*

Passion with a full orchestra, including the musically-gifted Paula on violin, supported by an eighty-strong choir. Kees conducted and Beatrice could be spotted in the middle of the choir, with some of the elder children towering over her much-diminished frame. For her this was an amazing experience, especially because as a child she had been forbidden by her Quaker parents from taking part in plays and concerts. (She did, however, confess to feeling a twinge of guilt the first time she attended the Passion Play at Oberammergau, as if she were being 'unfaithful' to her mother and father's memory.) But no-one, least of all Beatrice, could deny the importance of performing music together as a way of building spiritual fellowship during the dark times of the war.

*

Other life-affirming events for Beatrice at this time included the arrival of the first set of grandchildren. Paula and Paul had set up home in Amsterdam, but when Paula became pregnant the couple returned to Bilthoven so that the mother-to-be could give birth with the support of her mother and sisters. The young couple moved into the first floor of the *Eikenrode* building above the school. Helen and Henk were already living on the second floor and later Emma and Bart would live in part of the ground floor. On 7th December, 1940, Paula gave birth to a boy. He was named Daniel, after his uncle. Beatrice and Kees were almost as overjoyed as the new parents. The baby represented a sign of hope for the future, in spite of the bleak times ahead.

The following February, news reached the school staff of the rounding-up of Jewish men in Amsterdam, where German forces, armed with machine guns, had beaten and humiliated the men in the street, before deporting them to Buchenwald concentration camp. Children watched in terror and utter bewilderment as their fathers were suddenly snatched away and carted off, often never to be seen again.

*

At the end of 1941, Beatrice and Kees were due to mark their thirtieth wedding anniversary. In spite of the times of trial and challenge, particularly during the radical years of the 1920s, their love and mutual support for one another remained undiminished. They thought and acted as one.

As in all successful marriages, the couple complemented one another. He was the firebrand, the one to be found in the spotlight. Yet his commanding, and at times forbidding, presence was coupled with a mental fragility that made him liable to periods of dark depression. Beatrice was the bedrock during his low times; and, more, she was the inspiration for many of Kees's ideas. Although she would have been quick to deny it herself, Beatrice was in many ways wiser than her husband, and her calm intelligence made her a sensible counterbalance to his impetuousness. Her Quaker upbringing had imbued her with a strong sense of forbearance. To the children, their mother was a quiet presence in the background but Kees understood he would not have achieved the success of The Werkplaats without Beatrice's support and contributions. There was never any denying her deep devotion to her husband.

*

However, an issue was about to cause a rift between Beatrice and Kees that would threaten their seemingly unbreakable bond. (It said much about the strength of their marriage that each felt free to express their strong opinion and, ultimately, agree to disagree.)

In September, 1942, the German occupiers demanded that schools in Holland must give the names of all 'non-Aryan' children. And the initially conciliatory behaviour of the occupiers was replaced with warnings that there would be reprisals for disobeying the order.

This brought about a profound crisis in the minds of everyone at The Werkplaats. By this stage, the *Eikenrode* school had been forced to close with some of the Jewish children being transferred to a Dutch camp in North East Holland, Westerbork, where other Jewish refugees were being held to prevent them entering Holland. (The building had then been adapted for The Werkplaats kindergarten and as living quarters for the Boeke children.)

Other children from *Eikenrode* were now integrated into The Werkplaats. What should The Werkplaats do about the order to give the names of the Jewish children to the occupiers? Opinion was divided. To Beatrice and some others, to comply with the Nazis would have been entirely against the spirit of unity and brotherhood in the school; it would have been a betrayal of the whole community. Other people saw it differently. If the school was not seen to be co-operating with the occupiers' request it could mean The Werkplaats would have to close down and all the children would suffer as a consequence. Beatrice argued that closing the school down first would be a way of showing solidarity with the Jewish children *and* avoiding reprisals.

The others, including Kees, disagreed. The school should remain open. They argued that the act of just giving a list of names was comparatively harmless. Some of the Jewish children had managed to get false identity papers anyway. There would be time for the others to conveniently 'disappear' into the underground networks that had sprung up.

Beatrice wanted to wait and do nothing until the way became clearer. But it was decided to hand over the names of the Jewish children, in an act of expediency to enable The Werkplaats to stay open.

Later, Beatrice explained her reaction:

'I could *not* agree to this decision and with the other worker Jeanne Gallant [I] withdrew from co-operation with the WP [Werkplaats]. This decision cost me bitter sorrow but I saw no other way.'

For the first time in their lives together, Beatrice and Kees were no longer united in thought. For almost a year she refused to set foot in The Werkplaats. Her convictions, when tested, proved to be strong and vigorous.

The discord between the couple relaxed a little when they agreed Beatrice would give lessons at home to some of the Jewish children. And then Mirjam Waterman, who now had her own school at her parents' home in Loosdrecht, asked Beatrice if she would consider giving lessons there too. She was only too willing to say yes and cycled there twice a week, along with her colleague, Jeanne, giving lessons in English and French. (Beatrice was still reasonably fluent in French, it being one of her strongest subjects at school.) She found it a happy and fulfilling time but the school had to be abandoned when the Germans discovered its presence and decreed the children should be taken to Westerbork. The children scattered: many went into hiding with local families or went underground to be helped by the resistance movement involving Mirjam and Joop and Willie Westerweel, who were no longer at The Werkplaats. To Beatrice's great distress she did not hear from some of the children again.

Meanwhile, Beatrice was now a grandmother of three. In February of 1942, Helen's first child was born – a girl, Petronella, soon to be known as Nell. And in May of that year Emma gave birth to Marjon. They were all beautiful, treasured grandchildren.

That October Helen had a horrific accident. She was cycling through Bilthoven when she collided with a pedestrian and somersaulted over the bike's handlebars, cracking the base of her skull on the pavement. She was taken to the emergency department of St. Antonius hospital in Utrecht, with severe concussion and a serious fracture to her skull. For eight long weeks she had to stay there while Beatrice spent her time looking after baby Nell. Visiting Helen in hospital involved a long journey to Utrecht on a bus that was always crowded with German soldiers. Beatrice lived in absolute dread that they might discover she was in fact English and arrest her, and worse.

Beatrice was tense for another reason. She was harbouring a secret, which, if it were discovered, could jeopardise the entire family. She had taken in two young children to the Boeke household – a brother and a sister, who were Jewish.

*

Norman and Anita Magnus were aged nine and six when they were forced to flee the Dutch town of Breda where they lived, after the Germans invaded it in 1942. Breda had a very small Jewish population, of around 200 people, which made Jews all the more vulnerable. One of Anita's earliest memories was of having to wear a yellow star and not being allowed to use the buses. Gradually, she was aware of her Jewish friends 'disappearing' one-by-one. The Magnus family owed its survival to a tip-off from a sympathetic council employee, who told Anita's parents they must flee immediately or they would be deported to Auschwitz concentration camp. He would give them the compulsory identity papers (without the letter 'J' stamped on them, which would have marked them out as Jewish). They would have to change their names and adopt brand new identities. To make things a little easier for the children, their new surname would be 'Wachness', which sounded similar to Magnus. There were four children in all (Norman, Anita and their two younger sisters, Ingrid and Helga). Their mother and father asked them to pick new Dutch names for themselves. Norman became 'Jan', Anita chose 'Liesje', Ingrid became 'Lenie' and Helga picked 'Hennie'.

The whole family left Breda a day later, with the Germans already in pursuit. The children's parents told them that they were going to stay with families in the countryside, and under no account must they use their old names or real birthday dates or tell anybody they were Jewish. The children arrived in Bilthoven in October 1942. 'Jan' and 'Liesje' went to stay with Beatrice, Kees and the Boeke children still at home. Other children from The Werkplaats occasionally stayed with the Boekes, so the Magnus children were afforded some protection from suspicion. 'Jan' and 'Liesje' would stay in the Boeke household for the next two years. Their sisters, 'Lenie' and 'Hennie', were also in Bilthoven but they had to be moved around more frequently to avoid the German occupiers becoming suspicious. The little girls, only five and four, could not sustain the pretence as well as their older brother and sister.

At no time did Beatrice contemplate saying no to helping the Magnus children. She hated lies and deceit but she knew that the secrecy was essential to the survival of all of them. Her tactic was to say as little as possible to anyone, and simply to pretend the 'Wachness' children were Dutch. (It helped that they were fair-haired and had blue eyes.) Even her own children did not know their true identity. As for Kees, it would be impossible for him not to be aware of the story behind the arrival of the children, yet he appeared to have adopted a policy of deliberate blindness. He knew that if he asked no questions he would be told no lies. He and Beatrice simply did not discuss the matter. It was the best stratagem for them all.

In the meantime, Beatrice managed to provide a warm and stable environment for the Magnus children. It was safer for them if she did not tell them she knew they were Jewish. Nevertheless, the children went through great identity crises and 'Liesje', in particular, lived in terror of being found out and punished. Even when she fell off her bike and hurt herself, she was too scared to tell Beatrice what had happened, so afraid was she of being noticed. She still believed in a Santa Claus that punished naughty children and she suffered agonies in the lead-up to Christmas, 1942. Gradually, however, the Magnus children were integrated into school life in The Werkplaats. Unlike many Jewish children forced into hiding in cellars and attics for months, if not years, at least they were able to go to school and make friends, even if they had always to be on their guard.

The Magnusses were a tight-knit family, and, once a year, their parents managed to visit their children in Bilthoven. The two younger girls, 'Lenie' and 'Hennie', went to live with Emma, her husband Bart and baby Marjon for a time. Again the same secret policy had to be adhered to.

Publicly, Beatrice was still refusing to enter the Werkplaats, but a reconciliation came when Kees started a choir at the school which Jewish people were invited to attend. Beatrice felt able to become involved in the school's activities once more.

In Bilthoven the German Occupation tightened its grip. The Boekes and other adults had tried hard to keep life normal for the children. But by 1944 The Werkplaats school building was requisitioned by the Germans. The school staff desperately needed new premises and managed to find a spare classroom in the Christelijke (Christian) School nearby. Next to be requisitioned was *Eikenrode*, where Paula, Helen and Emma were living with their husbands and babies. News came also that the Boekes' house next door to the school was to be taken over. Beatrice and Kees moved to a large detached house on Gezichtlaan, with Candia (and later her fiancé, Gerard van Wijk), Theodora and Maya. There were a number of other children living with them, including the Magnus brother and sister, 'Jans' and 'Liesje'.

But the German forces were moving ever closer, rounding up the Jewish children with ruthless efficiency for deportation to Westerbork. One of the former Werkplaats teachers, Jet Kirpensteyn, told the chilling story of German soldiers who inspected the orphanage she now ran, asking her to remove the nappies of the male babies to see if they were circumcised (to prove that they were Jewish). Jet had a system for taking the Jewish children she was sheltering out in a boat on the nearby river while the inspection was carried out.

It was now so dangerous for the 'Wachness' children that they had to be moved on. They were smuggled to a farm and eventually all four children were reunited with their parents, where they managed to escape to safety. Other Jewish refugees were not so lucky. Some friends, the Nothman family, were captured and sent to Westerbork. Beatrice received a short postcard from them when they arrived. After that it was 'a silence that was never broken'.

By now the German forces were trying to capture all the young men in Holland, not just the Jewish men, for use in the German work camps. Beatrice and Kees lived in terror of their son, Daniel, or one of the sons-in-law, Paul, Bart, Henk or Gerard, being sent to the camps where they would be forced to work as slave labour in munitions factories, or repairing bomb-damaged roads or bridges, or helping food production by working on farms. Few of these labourers survived the brutality of the working conditions.

The young men had their own network of hiding places and all of them managed to avoid capture. But the strain for everybody was immense. When would the war ever end?

Beatrice and Kees's intention was to continue with school traditions as far as possible. Their bravest and most defiant act was to continue the summer camp experience that had been introduced in the 1930s and then suspended as the war in Holland started. Would it be possible for them to take The Werkplaats children on the same excursion?

In the summer of 1942 they took three school groups to the Veluwe parkland, which entailed great secrecy. In 1944 they wanted to do it again. The party included about 150 children and was a far riskier enterprise this time. Travelling by train was too dangerous as they were liable to be hit by machine-gun fire along the train route. Kees managed to obtain the use of three buses that left in convoy at four o'clock in the morning. Luckily, they all returned home in one piece, very much relieved but also uplifted by the experience.

By the winter of 1944, food was scarce in Holland, as in

the rest of Europe. Bread, meat and other basic foodstuffs were strictly rationed and every day of 'de Hongerwinter' ('Hunger Winter') was a struggle to find food. Beatrice, by now aged sixty, went out into the bitter cold each morning in search of firewood, and nettle and sorrel leaves to make soup. Candia found a field with potatoes and small turnips, which kept them going for a few weeks. Beetroot, made into soup, or served roasted was another mainstay. On one occasion Kees had gone out foraging for food but all he could find was tulip bulbs. Beatrice roasted them and the family learned to their surprise they had a similar taste to chestnuts. Food-wise, absolutely nothing would be wasted.

Beatrice was particularly concerned about the grandchildren and the nutritional needs of her two expectant daughters. Helen and Emma's babies were due in the New Year. Julia, Candia, Theodora and Maya went on a mission to find food for their sisters, cycling over seventy miles to friends in Barchem, coming back with precious rye (for bread), butter and eggs. Candia took the precaution of hiding the butter inside the leg of her trousers, where it melted and began trickling down her leg. Luckily, they managed to save the butter.

In spite of the cold dark winter, Beatrice found consolation in the way the family bonds strengthened during this period. There was no electricity, coal or gas at all – the only fuel was firewood – so the family spent their evenings together, huddled in blankets in the dark, save for a flicker of light from either a floating wick or an old bicycle lamp. In his fine orator's voice, Kees read Shakespeare to the gathered family members, transporting them out of their misery and into another world. At other times, the family conducted their choir rehearsals around the table.

As the New Year came, with no end in sight to the war, the safe arrival of two grandsons did much to cheer everyone. Emma gave birth to little Axel on 8th January, and nine days later Helen had Jan-Kees.

There were some narrow escapes in 1945. When Kees and

Beatrice were rehearsing a play with The Werkplaats children in the dining room of a Bilthoven hotel a squadron of airplanes flew over, dropping bombs before they careered away in the sky. One of the bombs landed so close that the building shook and the windows rattled terrifyingly as the children dropped to the floor. When they finally opened their eyes they were covered in plaster dust. It was a very close call.

But no episode came closer to chilling Beatrice's heart than when Kees and the school secretary, Stella, were taken into custody for questioning by the German Gestapo.

Beatrice would later learn that Stella had been woken and arrested at two o'clock in the morning. She was told by the German officers not to bother taking any possessions with her as she was going to be shot anyway.

Later that day, when Kees arrived at The Werkplaats, Stella was missing and three policemen were waiting to arrest him also. It transpired that a young lodger, who was Jewish, was living in Stella's house and he was a member of the Dutch Resistance. Stella had had her suspicions but had turned a blind eye. Meanwhile, Kees had not known anything about the man at all.

But unfortunately for Kees when he was arrested he was found to have a propaganda leaflet in his pocket that he had written, stating his declaration against the war. The very first section was headed in large letters, 'NO DICTATORSHIP', and the leaflet condemned the Nazi regime as 'scum' that had risen to the top.

The German police started to interrogate him about the Jewish lodger, who had committed a 'terrorist' act of sabotage in attempting to blow up a German train.

Kees stayed calm and, in his usual disarming manner, he began to talk with the policemen. He told them how ironic it was that twenty-five years ago, during the First World War, he had been arrested and deported from England for being 'pro-German', and now: "Here I am, and you're about to shoot me for being anti-German!"

Later, Beatrice was told that Kees had explained to the police his desire to live a life without force, one that demonstrated tolerance of others. His intention was to publish the leaflet after the war was over. The men had appeared to soften in their attitude, although they were still duty bound to report him.

Both Kees and Stella were taken to the SS headquarters in Utrecht where they awaited their execution.

Beatrice thought it would be the last time she would see her husband. She knew the reprisals for any person sheltering or assisting Jewish people would be swift and brutal. Joop Westerweel, the former Werkplaats principal had been captured and executed at Vught concentration camp for his resistance work. Colleagues who had witnessed Kees's arrest said he had appeared to show no fear; on the contrary, he looked strangely at peace. Beatrice felt utterly powerless. All she could do was to wait for news.

When Kees and Stella reached the prison, they heard that Stella's Jewish lodger was also there. As Kees was being taken to his cell he passed the lodger on the stairs, who whispered to Kees, "I told them you had nothing to do with it."

Stella was released first and sent back to Bilthoven, where she reported to Beatrice what had happened. The Jewish man was executed by firing squad. Kees was held for a further week – a time of agony for the family – but then suddenly was released without any explanation. He would later reflect that it was surely the Jewish man's testimony that Kees had not been involved that had saved his life.

That spring, in 1945, the Allies had made a concerted effort to push through Holland, and the German occupiers were already in retreat. Hitler's suicide on 30th April signalled the end of the rapidly-disintegrating Third Reich. News filtered through on 5th May that the Germans in Holland had surrendered to the Allies. After five interminable years of subjugation to the Nazi terror, the Dutch people were at last free. Although the people of Holland could breathe again, it would take months and years for them to start the healing process. For Beatrice and Kees, the only way they knew was to turn their attention back to the school.

*

The Werkplaats building was in a dire state by the time it was handed back. Immediately after the war, the building was occupied by British and Canadian troops until November, 1945, when, finally, it became available. Kees almost wept when he saw the chaotic state of it. Most of the furniture and equipment had been ransacked. What remained was unusable. Many of the teachers had scattered during the war. Joop Westerweel had already been executed; his wife Willie spent many months in Ravensbrück before her eventual release. Mirjam Waterman Pinkhof was captured and sent to Bergen Belsen, which she survived. Those teachers who remained at The Werkplaats had precious few resources left. Unless immediate financial help could be found, the school would have to close.

Two important background events were working in the school's favour during this period. Queen Wilhelmina, whom Kees had unsuccessfully petitioned over the tax issue during the 1920s, had appointed the former academic, Wim Schermerhorn, to serve as Prime Minister in the first post-war cabinet of June, 1945. By good fortune, Beatrice and Kees were already well acquainted with Prof Schermerhorn and his wife; the two Schermerhorn children had been students of The Werkplaats during the war. Thus the Prime Minister would be a useful strategic ally, Kees hoped.

And then Princess Juliana, the Queen's daughter, returned from her exile in Canada (where she had gone, following her escape to England). Whilst there, she, her husband and children had lived a normal, down-to-earth life, entirely free of the restraints of the monarchy. But now, having come back to Holland, Princess Juliana was determined her children would not be stifled within a rigid educational system that would transform her free-thinking children into royal puppets. She had heard of The Werkplaats school and was impressed by its unconventional yet seemingly successful pedagogic methods. She decided that the young princesses, Beatrix, Irene and Margriet, should attend The Werkplaats for their primary schooling, and she began making enquiries.

Beatrice and Kees were flabbergasted. To think that once they had been enemies of the state, and now their school and its ideology was being embraced by a member of the Royal family, no less. It was a novel experience to have friends in such high places – and too good an opportunity not to ask for financial support from the state in order to secure the school's future.

A generous government grant was promised and the couple began to look forward once again. The Werkplaats re-opened, having undergone only the most urgent repairs. Around 200 pupils were on roll, which brought in some revenue through school fees, but Kees was still hopeful of the emergency grant and possibly a state subsidy to enable a complete renovation of the school and the addition of extra buildings. In 1946, however, the Dutch Labour government was beaten in the general election and Kees and Beatrice had lost their key ally. The new Minister of Education agreed to honour the terms of the previous government, but, while Kees was away at educational conferences in Australia, New Zealand and America, the budget figures were revised and it was made clear that no money would be forthcoming. Kees returned to Bilthoven to start a vigorous campaign against the decision.

In December, 1946, the new government finally agreed to the emergency grant, providing the school would set up a board of trustees to administer the finances. It looked as if the school would be saved.

Meanwhile, Princess Juliana stayed true to her intentions and enrolled her daughters. The three princesses were driven each morning in a Cadillac sedan to The Werkplaats. Apart from their bodyguards and police dogs, the royal children entered fully into life at the school. Beatrix, aged eight, proved to be a talented artist and sculptor, with a passion for Van Gogh. Seven-year-old Irene, with her slender build, was well-suited to movement and dance – she particularly adored ballet and became proficient at it. Margriet, aged three, was happy playing with dolls in the kindergarten wing. All children at The Werkplaats were expected to perform cleaning chores, as well as taking their turn on the cooking rota, and the princesses were no exception. (When the girls were later featured in LIFE magazine, the journalist visiting The Werkplaats was surprised to see Princess Beatrix in the school kitchen with tears rolling down her cheeks – she was peeling onions in preparation for school lunch.)

Beatrice and Kees were now confident their school would attract a state subsidy. An important condition was attached to the subsidy, however. The Werkplaats would have to undergo some fundamental changes to the way it operated to enable it to 'fit in' as a legally-recognised school within the Dutch state school system. Otherwise, the offer of the subsidy would be withdrawn. So, for the final time, the battle lines were drawn between the Boekes and the state. It seemed they were being asked to make an impossible choice: to abandon the first principles on which The Werkplaats was based, or to refuse to comply, knowing it would be the end of their life's work.

Ever since its humble beginnings as a home school in the 1920s, The Werkplaats had operated with complete freedom from government regulations. The school managed its own teaching without conforming to a prescribed syllabus. The only qualification needed by its teachers was a belief in the principles of progressive education. The school managed its own scarce finances. Pupils, or 'Workers', did not take the national exams required for university entrance.

In short, the Werkplaats was not a 'legal' school according to state regulations.

In order to be granted the subsidy, the school would have to change with regards to two major aspects: teacher qualifications and state matriculation examinations. All Werkplaats teachers on a salary would have to have full state qualifications. And, even more difficult to accept, was the requirement that the children would have to take the exams set by the state, exams which Kees considered inferior to the Werkplaats Test System that had been developed over the years.

As usual he turned to Beatrice for advice. She was always an excellent sounding board.

They discussed, somewhat ruefully, how once upon a time they would have taken to the streets in protest. They would have fought the state system directly, even being willing to go to prison for their beliefs.

"I *was* a naughty boy back then, wasn't I?" Kees said.

But their radical years were long over. Their uncompromising sense of conviction had now mellowed, and, although they had lost none of their original fire, they could now accept that sometimes it was better to compromise, to work from within, rather than setting themselves outside society.

Following further discussions with The Werkplaats staff, they decided the school should comply. Kees made the point that he considered the ruling a temporary one and he would be campaigning to make the current state regulations bend to The Werkplaats model, rather than the other way round.

A building was found to provide the base for the new school. Ironically, it was the site of a training centre built by the German occupiers. The building was comprehensively renovated, a new storey added, and the acres of land surrounding the building were converted into playing fields. Kees and Beatrice watched the building take shape.

The school had already restarted after the war but the opening of the brand new building on 6th January, 1951, was a symbolic choice. It marked exactly twenty-five years since Kees and his four young daughters had marched down the lane from *Het Boschhuis* to their 'home school', none of them, least of all Beatrice, with any inkling of the struggles and triumphs that were still to come.

Postscript:
As the days go by,
1951-1976

Beatrice and Kees continued to travel around the world, with Kees contributing to educational conferences on progressive education. The Werkplaats began its programme of modifications and the Boekes were forced to take a pragmatic view of the changes in the school. Kees retired from The Werkplaats on his seventieth birthday in 1954, where a huge party was held to celebrate the work that he and Beatrice had done. The Werkplaats school continued to flourish. Not only did it achieve respectability, it also acquired a certain snob value. Parents became desperate to send their children to the school. To this day, the school still thrives, albeit as a more conventional school than it had originally been and now fully compliant with the Dutch education system. Beatrice and Kees became regarded in educational circles as two of the most original and exceptional educators of the twentieth century, in Holland and around the world.

Even in retirement, Beatrice and Kees remained full of vigour. Beatrice had never given up her dream of returning to Syria one day. She and Kees wanted to try and replicate the model of an International Children's Community for underprivileged and refugee children in the Middle East. The couple spent eight months in Lebanon trying to raise funding for the project. Sadly, they were unable to find a local group to sponsor the scheme and Kees and Beatrice also suffered ill health, forcing them to return to Holland.

'To our great disappointment, our hopes were not fulfilled,' Beatrice said.

In 1955 they settled in Abcoude, just outside Amsterdam. Beatrice's ambition was to make their home the centre of family life, where their children and grandchildren would often come. 'How thankful I should be if our Abcoude home might become "Daar e Salaam" – "The House of Peace".'

The Boeke children followed different paths; some went far away while others stayed near. After a long illness, Daniel left for America with his new wife, Lis. Emma and Bart emigrated to Canada with their children, Marjon, Axel and Beatrice. The other Boeke daughters stayed in Holland, and a number of grandchildren attended The Werkplaats. All of them married, apart from Julia and Maya. Between the children, Beatrice and Kees had thirteen grandchildren. They were proud and loving grandparents.

On their travels the couple met Walter and Irene Laffan and the four became close and dear friends. Walter described the Boekes with great affection: 'Kees the pioneer spirit, Kees the perpetual child, and Betty the incarnation of mother love, who at the same time goes out to our open-air bathing pool and takes an early morning dip at the end of October!' Beatrice's love of the outdoors remained.

In July, 1966, Kees Boeke died. Tributes poured in for this passionate, some would say quixotic, man. He was, at times, disillusioned, often depressed and in the later stages of his life, a sufferer of Alzheimer's, but his passion and belief had shaped his life and that of his family immeasurably.

Beatrice outlived him for a considerable time. After his death, she wrote an account that was printed in Dutch of her husband's life: 'Het Leven van Kees Boeke' (The Life of Kees Boeke). She also translated a key text of his on the principles of Sociocracy into English, called 'Sociocracy: Democracy As It Might Be'.

She enjoyed travelling with her daughters to England and Israel, and to see Emma in Canada and Daniel in New Jersey. She was particularly excited about travelling by plane.

Beatrice's spiritual faith remained as strong as ever. Although she had resigned from the Society of Friends in the 1920s, she felt Quakerism was her true spiritual home. She became a much-valued member of the Amsterdam Quaker Meeting in her later years, attending every week. Her friend and former Werkplaats scholar, Pieter Ketner, paid tribute to a 'wonderful' woman, who, typically, would stay in the background but always impressed him with her quiet integrity and the profound wisdom and intelligence she brought to discussions. Beatrice's commitment to peace and social justice never wavered. In 1969, at the age of eighty-five, she joined the demonstrations against the American war in Vietnam.

On her 90th birthday, in 1974, her children organised an enormous family party for her. Julia Boeke wrote to the Boeke Trust for a financial contribution, which it was glad to supply. Beatrice found it a wonderful occasion being surrounded by children, grandchildren and great-grandchildren. In honour of her birthday, a former pupil from the Werkplaats, who was now a horticulturalist, named his first rose after her.

Beatrice Cadbury died on 13th February, 1976, following a short illness, at her home in Abcoude. She was 91. Beatrice's obituary in the Friends' magazine paid tribute to a loving woman, who 'saw the best in everyone'. Her long-time friend and Werkplaats Helper, Lois A. Brown, said Beatrice's enduring message was that 'Love never faileth'.

Following Beatrice's death, the Bournville Pensioners Association (one of the many groups to have benefited from Boeke Trust funds) suggested a short account of the Boeke Trust be written to pay tribute to the lives and ideals of Beatrice and Kees Boeke. Details of the booklet can be found in the bibliography.

Visitors to the Yad Vashem Museum in Jerusalem will be able to see the names of Kees and Betty Boeke on the 'Righteous Among the Nations' wall of honour. This award commemorated the couple posthumously for their bravery in sheltering Jewish children at the school and in their home at the height of the Nazi occupation of Holland. One of those children, Anita Magnus Frank, ('Liesje'), described the Boeke family as 'magnificent' and Beatrice as a 'loving, caring ... oh, unbelievably wonderful woman'.

Beatrice's legacy continues in many other ways. The peace groups, the IFOR and War Resisters' International (formerly PACO), which held their inaugural meetings at the 'house in the woods' in Bilthoven are still going strong.

In the 1970s, Beatrice wrote a biography of her mother, 'Emma Richard Cadbury, 1846-1907'. In the book she stressed the importance of keeping her mother and father's story alive for future descendants. The final lines of that work are a fitting end to this account of Beatrice's own life.

'May the story of their lives shine as a glow from the past and a star of hope for the future.'

*

Bibliography

BOOKS

Alexander, H.C. and Kennedy Maclean, J. (1995) *A Romance of Song and Soul-winning* 'Tennessee': Sword of the Lord Publishers

Alexander-Dixon, H.C. (1906) *Richard Cadbury of Birmingham* [Unknown Binding]

Bartlett, P.W. (1960) *Barrow Cadbury: A Memoir* [Unknown binding]

Bell, J. (Ed.) (1935) *We Did Not Fight 1914-18 Experiences of War Resisters* London: Sheppard and Allen

Boeke-Cadbury, B. (1970) Emma Richard Cadbury: 1846-1907 [Unknown Binding]

Boeke-Cadbury, B. (1971) *Het Leven van Kees Boeke* [Unknown Binding]

Cadbury, D. (2010) *Chocolate Wars* London: HarperPress

Chinn, C. (1998) *The Cadbury Story: A Short History* Warwickshire: Brewin Books

Crosfield, J. (1985) *A History of the Cadbury Family* [Unknown Binding]

Fast, V.K. (2011) *Children's Exodus: A History of the Kindertransport* London: I.B. Tauris

Fox, S. (1989) *Helen Cadbury and Charles M. Alexander: A Love that Embraced the World* London: Marshall Pickering

Graham, J.W. (1922) *Conscription and Conscience* London: George Allen and Unwin

Insull, T. (1978) *The Boeke Trust in Brief* Birmingham [Unknown Binding]

Kuipers, H.J. (1992) *De wereld als werkplaats: Over de vorming van Kees Boeke en Beatrice Cadbury* [Unknown Binding]

Page, K. (1921) *The Sword or the Cross* The Christian Century Press

Prasad, D. (2005) *War is a crime against humanity: the story of War Resisters' International* London: War Resisters' International

Rawson, W. (1956) *Kees and Betty Boeke: A Short Account of their Lives and Work* [Unknown Binding]

Rawson, W. (1956) *The Werkplaats Adventure: An account of Kees Boeke's great pioneer comprehensive, its methods and psychology* London: Vincent Stuart

Rigby, A. (1988) *A Life in Peace: Biography of Wilfred Wellock* Prism Press

Sturge, W.H. and Clark, T. (1931) *The Mount School York* London and Toronto: J.M. Dent and Sons Ltd.

Wallis, J. (1991) *Valiant for Peace: History of the Fellowship of Reconciliation, 1914-1989* London: The Fellowship of Reconciliation

Whitcut, J. (1976) *Edgbaston High School: 1876-1976* Birmingham: Governors of Edgbaston High School

Wilmot, F. and P. Saul (1998) *A Breath of Fresh Air: Birmingham's Open-Air Schools 1911-1970* Chichester: Phillimore

ARCHIVED MATERIAL

MINUTES of THE BOEKE TRUST MEETINGS 1922-1935
retrieved from The Bournville Archives, Birmingham

KEES BOEKE ARCHIVE retrieved from The International
Institute for Social History, Amsterdam

Boxes 1-100 Personal letters and correspondence of the
Cadbury family and Kees Boeke

Box 169-170 'Memories of my childhood and girlhood, of my married
life and its various vicissitudes' (rough copy with corrections) by Beatrice
Boeke-Cadbury, May 1956

INTERNET MATERIAL

Transcript of Interview with Anita Magnus Frank, 4 January
1990, United States Holocaust Memorial Museum. Retrieved
from: http://collections.ushmm.org/artifact/image/h00/00/
h0000071.pdf

'Sociocracy: Democracy as It Might Be' by Kees Boeke (1884-
1966), Version translated by Beatrice Cadbury Boeke. Retrieved
from: http://www.socionet.us/blog/2010/11/07/sociocracy-democracy-
as-it-might-be-by-kees-boeke-1884-1966/

The Fellowship of Reconciliation, The Cambridge Review, December
1984, by John Ferguson. Retrieved from: http://www.ifor.org/
articles/IFOR_history_by_J._Ferguson_1984_-_REVISED.pdf

MAGAZINES

LIFE, 3 April 1950, 'Princesses at Work: Three royal daughters
of Holland are learning about Sociocracy,' by David Perlman

INTERVIEWS CARRIED OUT (face to face, telephone and email)

Candia Boeke, Daniela Hooghiemstra, Dr. Philip Rumke, Lis Boeke, Pieter Ketner, Tjeerd Dibbets

Acknowledgements

I am indebted to many, many people, who have each been instrumental in helping me to start and complete this book:

Mike Byrne, of Acocks Green Library, who helped me track down the earliest source material on Beatrice Cadbury.

Hans Jan Kuipers, who very kindly sent me an English summary of his PhD thesis on the Werkplaats School.

Nicola Monaghan, Jackie Gay and Richard Beard, my Graduate Diploma in Writing tutors at Birmingham City University, who helped me shape the book in its early stages. Your comments, insights and guidance on the publishing industry were invaluable.

My writing friends, Kathleen Dixon Donnelly, Nick Le Mesurier, Roger Noble, Brenda Baxter, Emma Whittle and Rob Ronsson, who commented on my early experimental drafts, came to talks, or were, generally, 'champions' for Beatrice.

David Viner, of Solihull Libraries, for very ably promoting my Beatrice Cadbury talks throughout Solihull and beyond.

Tricia Wombell, for her early support of the book, on her blog and in LIME magazine.

Jon Price of the Made in Birmingham website, for his early support.

Staff from Birmingham Central Library, who assisted me in searching the Cadbury family archives.

Staff from the Woodbrooke Quaker Study Centre, especially Ian Jackson and Sandra Berry, who provided access to the library.

Sarah Foden, Jackie Jones and the staff from the Bournville Archives, who could not have been more welcoming or helpful to me.

Ella Molenaar, and her colleagues at the International

Institute of Social History in Amsterdam, for seeking permission on my behalf to consult the Kees Boeke Archive, and for assisting me so tirelessly during my research visit.

Chris Petitt and Henrica Takens-Milne, whose valiant efforts to connect me with the Dutch Quakers paid off in ways I never dreamed of.

Pieter Ketner and Tjeerd Dibbets, who warmly welcomed me to the Amsterdam Quaker meeting for a happy afternoon of Werkplaats reminiscences.

Candia Boeke, for generously granting me a telephone interview, in spite of her poor health. Thank you for providing the highlight of my research.

Dr. Philip Rumke, with whom I shared many emails and who made enquiries for me and provided me with valuable contacts.

Daniela Hooghiemstra, who is writing Kees Boeke's biography, and who generously shared her insights into Kees and 'Betty'.

Lis Boeke, for sharing her memories of her late husband, Daniel Boeke, and her mother-in-law, 'Betty'.

Annelies and Hans Kamerbeek, for a memorable visit to a very special house. My family and I will always remember your kindness in welcoming a group of strangers into your home.

Mike Albutt, Margaret Sharp and the Property Committee of Acocks Green Methodist Church, for allowing me a quiet space to write during the final stages of the book. Your good wishes and cups of tea sustained me no end.

The production of this book would not have been possible without the help of three first-rate publishing professionals, who were a pleasure to work with:

Clare Christian, my editor, who did a sterling job of helping me with the manuscript when it was still in draft form.

Stuart Bache, who designed both the book and ebook covers.

Adam Davis, who typeset the book.

And finally, thanks to my loved ones – Peter, Anna and Stella. I am truly blessed to have your constant love and support.

Lightning Source UK Ltd.
Milton Keynes UK
UKOW051141230212

187796UK00001B/7/P